THE SAVED

A Former Atheist's *Guide to* Christianity

JADE CREIGHTON

Cover design: Jade Creighton
Back cover photo: Kathy Hollick

Printed in the United States of America

ISBN: 979-8-218-31650-1

ACKNOWLEDGEMENTS

A special thank you to the Father, Son and Holy Spirit, for guiding and instructing me throughout the process of compiling this book;

To my husband, Chad Creighton, for your encouragement and support, and for choosing me to be your wife;

To my sister, Amber Wardia, for inspiring me to write this because of your own creativity and perseverance in writing;

And to my sister-in-Christ, Diana Boyce, for teaching me to abide in the Lord, and for showing me that all things are possible with Christ Jesus.

CONTENTS

RECOVERED FROM ATHEISM

My name is Jade Creighton and I am an ex-atheist. I am not a trained author, Bible scholar, or expert. I'm just an average person who lived in the world as a non-believer for a long time, and then suddenly had to figure out how to be a Christian.

Being a former atheist, I couldn't relate to good Christians who only messed up once in a while. **I wanted realistic advice for imperfect, dysfunctional Christians (like me) who messed up constantly.** I was used to being "bad." I had lived most of my life without a moral compass, and I had some questions:

-Is it even possible for someone like me to live the Christian life?
-Is this really something I want to commit to?
-Will people think I've gone crazy?
-Am I going to have to change my personality and stop doing the things I enjoy?

Regardless of whether you're a new believer, or if you've been a believer for a while and you still have some questions, this book is for you.

Have you ever felt like…

…You want to be a good person, but the damage is already done and you will never be normal?

…You want to unlearn the bad habits and traits you picked up in the past, but it seems impossible because they are so ingrained in you?

…Your dysfunctional past defines who you are, and in becoming a Christian you will lose your identity?

…You're afraid of becoming too "churchy" and alienating your friends and family?

I believe I have put together an easy-to-read guide that might save you some frustration on your journey, written by someone who has been on that journey. This guide will show you what the Bible has to say about a variety of challenging topics, and how to apply that knowledge in your own life.

Inside this book you will find several features to help you, including:

Did-You-Know Facts,
Personal Testimonials, and
Actionable Insights…

… That you can begin to use right now to get real results.

The purpose of this book is to offer you encouragement and practical advice on your journey as a Christian. This is a collection of some of the most valuable and useful information that I've gathered on my own journey, but your journey is uniquely yours; so ask, seek, knock, and go where the Lord takes you.

> "Ask and it will be given to you; seek and you will find; knock and the door will be opened to you. For everyone who asks receives; the one who seeks finds; and to the one who knocks, the door will be opened."
> Matthew 7:7-8 (NIV)

DON'T LISTEN TO ME

There is no substitute for knowing the Word of God. Scriptures can be twisted, manipulated, and taken out of context in attempt to confuse and trick us. The only way to defend against this is to study God's Word directly from the Bible, and to know it for yourself.

Don't automatically believe what people tell you is (or isn't) in the Bible. This goes for any person, preacher, friend, relative, spouse, church, or book. Even this book. Go directly to the source and look up everything for yourself. It's ok to ask questions and to use Bible study tools – but always allow God to take you on your own journey through His written Word.

Reading the Bible can be challenging, but there are three important steps you can take beforehand for a more fruitful and enjoyable experience (*See Chapter 13, How to Read the Bible*):

1. **Ask, seek, and knock.** You don't have to be a Bible scholar to understand God's Word! Begin your Bible-reading journey with the desire to gain understanding. God has the ability to reveal His Word supernaturally.

2. **Pray.** Activate your connection with God. Ask Him for guidance and wisdom as you read and study His Word.

3. **Get the right Bible**. Get a Bible that you actually enjoy reading.

ACTIONABLE INSIGHT

Do not trust what others tell you is
in the Bible. Read it yourself.

CHAPTER 1

PRAYER FOR RECEIVING CHRIST

Are you ready to commit or re-commit your life to Christ? How will you know?

If you've already asked yourself this question, then you are ready to give your life to Christ. It doesn't matter what you have done, what you are doing, or how bad and unforgivable you might think that you are. **There are no prerequisites for giving your life to Christ.** Here's what the Bible says about it:

> "If you confess with your mouth Jesus as Lord, and believe in your heart that God raised Him from the dead, you will be saved; for with the heart a person believes, resulting in righteousness, and with the mouth he confesses, resulting in salvation…for everyone who calls on the name of the Lord will be saved."
> Romans 10:9-10,13 (NASB)

Admitting that we need Jesus can be difficult and uncomfortable, especially when we first start out. Sometimes it might feel weird or embarrassing. The freedom and comfort come when we know that we can count on Him, and that He is true to His Word (the Bible) which says:

-With God, all things are possible. (Matthew 19:26)

-Nothing can separate us from the love of God in Christ. (Romans 8:38-39)

-Who Jesus sets free, is free indeed. (John 8:36)

Now go to a quiet space where you can be alone with the Lord, and where you won't feel embarrassed talking to Him out loud.

> "But when you pray, go into your most private room, close the door and pray to your Father who is in secret, and your Father who sees [what is done] in secret will reward you." Matthew 6:6 (AMP)

Prayer for committing your life to Christ:

Jesus, I admit that I need You. I declare that You are my Lord and Savior. I believe that You died on the cross for me and rose again. I want you to come into my life and into my heart. Please forgive me, change my life, and show me how to know You. Thank You for the gift of salvation. In the name of Jesus, Amen.

CHAPTER 2

HOW TO PRAY

Praying isn't just a boring obligation that we must do at nighttime while kneeling at our bedsides. **Prayer is an essential part of our walk with Christ.** It's the way that we connect to God through Jesus. It's how we spend time in the Heavenly Places. It's how we stand against the devil.

God hears our prayers and cares about the details of our lives. When Jesus died on the cross, the veil which separated God's dwelling place in the temple was torn, symbolizing a sufficient atonement for sin and making the way to God open to all people (Matthew 27:45-55, *The Death of Jesus*). **Because of Jesus' sacrifice, we are now able to pray to God directly through our intercessor, Jesus Christ.**

DID YOU KNOW?

Before Jesus died on the cross, only the elect high priests were allowed to communicate with God. People would have to make their request to the high priest, and then the high priest would go into The Holiest of Holies (the place where God dwelled within the temple) and speak to God on their behalf.[1] (Hebrews 9:1-10)

However, God is not a magic genie in a lamp, waiting around to grant us wishes. Just because we ask for something in prayer does NOT mean we will get it.

The book of James gives us a little more insight. James is addressing believing Christians who are trying to achieve their selfish goals without asking God, or by asking God wrongly.

"What causes quarrels and what causes fights among you? Is it not this, that your passions are at war within you? You desire and do not have, so you murder. You covet and cannot obtain, so you fight and quarrel. **You do not have,**

because you do not ask. You ask and do not receive, because you ask wrongly, to spend it on your passions." James 4:1-3 (ESV)

The Truth Of God Vs. How We Feel

The Word of God is the truth – but we don't always want to hear the truth. Even when the truth hurts, sometimes all we need is a little tough love to nudge us in the right direction. The Word of God doesn't change, even though the world around us does. Society changes, cultural norms change, even we change – **but God's Word remains the same yesterday, today, and forever** (Hebrews 13:8).

Our prayers are answered when they align with God's will and timing, for His glory and for our good. That's why we can't necessarily pray for wealth and get it, because only God knows what is best for each of us. There are things we can pray for that we already know God has promised to us, because they are in the Bible. For example, one thing I have prayed for and never been denied is a deeper understanding of God's Word.

"Blessed is the one who finds wisdom, and the one who gets understanding, for the gain from her is better than gain from silver and her profit better than gold. She is more precious than jewels, and nothing you desire can compare with her. Long life is in her right hand; in her left hand are riches and honor. Her ways are ways of pleasantness, and all her paths are peace. She is a tree of life to those who lay hold of her; those who hold her fast are called blessed." Proverbs 3:13-18 (ESV)

The Lord's Prayer

Matthew 6:9-14 is commonly referred to as The Lord's Prayer, because Jesus Himself teaches us a lesson on how to pray. Here are Jesus' instructions:

"Pray then like this:

'Our Father in heaven,
hallowed be your name.
Your kingdom come,
your will be done,
on earth as it is in heaven.
Give us this day our daily bread,
and forgive us our debts,
as we also have forgiven our debtors.
And lead us not into temptation,
but deliver us from evil.'

For if you forgive others their trespasses, your heavenly Father will also forgive you, but if you do not forgive others their trespasses, neither will your Father forgive your trespasses." Matthew 6:9-15 (ESV)

Even as an atheist I had heard of the Lord's Prayer. These verses can be rote for some, but what do they actually mean? Here is a simple breakdown of each line:

-Dear God in Heaven
-Your Name is, was, and will always be Holy
-We pray for Jesus' return
-Your way is always the best way
-In this life and the next
-Please take care of us today
-We are sorry when we don't listen to you
-Help us to love and to forgive one another
-Help us to resist the devil
-You are the God Most High for all eternity

<u>Easy Prayer Recipe</u>

"Be anxious for nothing, but in everything by prayer and supplication, with thanksgiving, let your requests be made known to God." Philippians 4:6 (NKJV)

Praying with forethought and intention can get your prayer life on track and deepen your relationship with the Lord. Whether you are in a prayer closet with notebooks full of prayer requests or praying quietly during your morning commute, there are some key components that are helpful to include in your prayers (based on Matthew 6:9-14 and Philippians 4:6, above):

(**Thanksgiving** + **Supplication** + **Exaltation** + **God's Word** + **Name of Jesus**) = A SOLID PRAYER

- **Thanksgiving** – Begin your prayers from a place of gratitude. Thank God for some things. If you are praying for someone, thank God for that person.

- **Supplication** – Make your requests sincere, humble and genuine.

- **Exaltation** – State the awesomeness of who God is.

- **God's Word** – Repeat God's Word back to Him by referring to scripture.

- **Name of Jesus** – There is power in the name of Jesus! End prayers with the words "in the name of Jesus."

Here is an example in a prayer for you, dear reader:

> *Lord, thank You for the reader of this prayer. Thank you for their willingness and desire to get to know You better. Thank You for connecting us through Your Word. You are the Author and Creator of all things, weaving the grand tapestry that brings us all together. Thank You, Lord, that we can pray to You directly because of what Jesus did on the cross. Lord, bless us and keep us. Make our paths straight and guide us in Your ways. May we have a closer relationship with You through Your Word, which says that 'blessed is the one who finds wisdom and gains understanding.' Give us Your wisdom and a deeper understanding of Your Word. Thank You for Your written Word, that we may study it freely. Thank You for loving us and for caring about the details of our lives. In the name of Jesus, Amen.*

<u>Mealtime Prayer</u>

Bless your food – because you never know exactly where it came from, who touched it, or how it's prepared. Mealtime prayers aren't just another one of those boring obligations; they are an opportunity to thank the Lord, and your food will be blessed as a result.

Lord, thank You for this meal. Please bless it in Your name, and all of the hands involved in bringing it to our table. May it nourish our bodies, in the name of Jesus. Amen.

Talking To God

You don't have to use any prayer formula to talk to God. Go before Him and tell Him how you feel. Go to God *first* with your thoughts and concerns, before going to anyone else. Talk to Him as you would your best friend, letting your guard down and being authentic. Jesus tells us to become as little children: Innocent, honest, humble, and teachable.

> "Whoever humbles himself like this child is the greatest in the kingdom of heaven." Matthew 18:4 (ESV)

Sometimes I talk to God throughout the day, chumming it up and making observations. He's always there and He always has time for me. But sometimes when I'm going through hardships and I feel broken, I need to sit on His lap and cry like a baby. Jesus is the Comforter, so we can cry to Him and tell Him everything that is bothering us. This goes for men and women, young and old. We are never a burden on Him, or taking up too much of His time. He is Omnipresent (everywhere all at once) so we never have to schedule an appointment with Him or wait in line.

Listening To God

It's easier for most of us to talk to God rather than to listen to Him; however, there are some things to take notice of when God is trying to get our attention:

Resonating Within

Have you ever felt suddenly moved or stirred by a certain topic? Is there something that is resonating within you when you think about a particular sermon or area of scripture?

Hearing the Same Thing Over and Over

Have you ever heard the same message over and over again? Maybe a particular scripture stirred something up for you, then you heard the same message again in some song lyrics, then your eye caught an article about it. Everything happens for a reason. The Bible says that all things work together for God's glory and for our good as believers, so if you hear the same Biblical message over and over again, it's probably a good idea to pay attention.

> "And we know that all things work together for good to those who love God, to those who are the called according to His purpose." Romans 8:28 (NKJV)

Being Still

Sometimes we pray and ask and give thanks, and then we rush off to continue on with our day. How often do we just wait and listen? For many of us, being still and waiting is one of the most difficult things to do. It might feel counterintuitive, but it's important to humble ourselves and get down on our knees before the Lord once in a while – not only figuratively, but literally. Physical prayer positions, like kneeling, are conducive to being still and waiting on the Lord. Your particular prayer position and how often you do it is up to you. Sometimes it takes practice, but it may also take humility, so you can go into your 'prayer closet' for some privacy:

> "But when you pray, go into your most private room, close the door and pray to your Father who is in secret, and your Father who sees [what is done] in secret will reward you." Matthew 6:6 (AMP)

CHAPTER 3

DECISION MAKING

One of the qualities of highly successful businesspeople is the innate ability to make the right decisions quickly. It's as if they "just know" what to do. Yet, not everyone has that ability. How, then, should we go about making decisions, and how do we know whether or not they are the right ones?

You and I don't have to be highly successful businesspeople in order to know how to make the right decisions, because we are now children of the God Most High and ambassadors of the Lord Jesus Christ. God has given us the Holy Spirit and His written Word to help us understand the difference between right and wrong. When our choices and decisions align with the Word of God, we can trust that they are the right ones. But how do we know for sure that our choices and decisions are aligning with the will of God?

Ask God First

All decision making should begin with prayer. One of the best things about having a relationship with Jesus is the ability to access God directly through prayer. Who better to ask for guidance and advice than the All-Knowing God of the Universe? We tend to make decisions and do things of our own accord, asking the Lord to bless them afterwards. What we should be doing is going to Him first and asking *permission*. We can include the Lord in our decision making from the start by praying before we do anything, asking for God's advice (as well as His permission to proceed).

DID YOU KNOW?

God is:

Omnipotent

Almighty; All-Powerful

Omnipresent

Everywhere all at once

Omniscient

All-Knowing; Infinitely Wise[1]

It might feel weird to ask God's permission to do something, but it helps to remember that He really does know best. There is a saying, "Let go and let God," which means to trust in the Lord by letting go (of our fears, doubts, desire to control outcomes, etc.) and allowing God to work.

Doors

Have you ever heard that when God closes one door, He opens another? Pray and ask for doors to be opened that will draw you nearer to the Lord, and for doors to be closed that may distract you away from Him.

- Pray in detail (about the specifics of your situation)
- Pray from a big picture/eternal lens (how will this affect your walk with the Lord?)
- Pray for discernment (understanding God's will)
- Pray for patience (while you wait on the Lord)

Unanswered Prayers

Once you get used to it, praying is the easy part. The difficulty for many of us is waiting patiently on the Lord and accepting that everything happens in God's own time, and in God's own way. Sometimes, our prayers are answered in ways that we don't expect; sometimes they don't seem like they are being answered at all.

How do we know if our prayers are being answered?

1. **Trust in the Lord and know that all things work together for your good.**

> "And we know that all things work together for good **to those who love God, to those who are the called according to His purpose**." Romans 8:28 (NKJV)

It's like they say on those business remodeling shows: Trust the process. We've got to trust in the Lord while He works things out. It's one of the ways we can put our faith into action. We might have to deal with people or go through situations that we don't like, but we know we can bear it in the meantime because God is working things out for our good.

2. **Do your due diligence.**

Even though it can be hard to let go of control, our job ultimately is to abide in Christ – and the best way to know if we are abiding in Christ is to study the Word of God. The Bible doesn't just provide us with moral guidelines; it reveals God's heart and character, giving us an opportunity to get to know Him, as well as His expectations of us.

The scriptures tell us that when we abide in Christ (wait on, remain in, continue with, live by) and pray according to God's will, God hears us and whatever we ask will be done:

> "Abide in me, and I in you. As the branch cannot bear fruit by itself, unless it abides in the vine, neither can you, unless you abide in me. I am the vine; you are the branches. Whoever abides in me and I in him, he it is that bears much fruit, **for apart from me you can do nothing**. If anyone does not abide in me he is thrown away like a branch and withers; and the branches are gathered, thrown into the fire, and burned. **If you abide in me, and my words abide in you, ask whatever you wish, and it will be done for you**." John 15:4-7 (ESV)

> "And this is the confidence that we have toward him, **that if we ask anything according to his will he hears us.** And if we know that he hears us in whatever we ask, **we know that we have the requests that we have asked of him**." 1 John 5:14-15 (ESV)

3. **Know that God will answer your prayers in His own way, in His own timing.**

Be patient while you wait on the Lord. If it seems like your prayers are not being answered, **give God a chance to work on you while you wait, allowing yourself the opportunity to be tested.**

> "Do not be conformed to this world, but be transformed

by the renewal of your mind, **that by testing you may discern what is the will of God,** what is good and acceptable and perfect." Romans 12:2 (ESV)

"**But they who wait for the Lord shall renew their strength;** they shall mount up with wings like eagles; they shall run and not be weary; they shall walk and not faint." Isaiah 40:31 (ESV)

"**Be still before the Lord and wait patiently for him**; fret not yourself over the one who prospers in his way, over the man who carries out evil devices! Refrain from anger, and forsake wrath! **Fret not yourself; it tends only to evil.** For the evildoers shall be cut off, but those who wait for the Lord shall inherit the land." Psalm 37:7-9 (ESV)

"Wait for the Lord; be strong, and **let your heart take courage;** wait for the Lord!" Psalm 27:14 (ESV)

<u>Triple Stamp It, No Erasies</u>

If you've trusted the Lord, prayed, and waited patiently – then stick with your decision. Don't go back and agonize over "what ifs". If you've done your due diligence, then you can trust that your decision was the right one. If you've already gotten an answer, don't doubt whether or not you really got that answer. When our decisions lead us to tough situations, remember that there is a season for everything:

"For everything there is a season, and a time for every matter under heaven:

a time to **be born**, and a time to **die**;
a time to **plant**, and a time to **pluck up** what is planted;
a time to **kill**, and a time to **heal**;
a time to **break down**, and a time to **build up**;
a time to **weep**, and a time to **laugh**;
a time to **mourn**, and a time to **dance**;
a time to **cast away stones**, and a time to **gather stones**

together;
a time to **embrace**, and a time to **refrain from embracing**;
a time to **seek**, and a time to **lose**;
a time to **keep**, and a time to **cast away**;
a time to **tear**, and a time to **sew**;
a time to **keep silence**, and a time to **speak**;
a time to **love**, and a time to **hate**;
a time for **war**, and a time for **peace**."
Ecclesiastes 3:1-8 (ESV)

Yes, You Are Allowed To Change Your Mind

We are allowed to make decisions and then re-examine those decisions – as long as we are looking to God for our answers and not to ourselves. We should never make decisions (or avoid making decisions) out of fear. There are a number of verses in the Bible instructing us not to fear, but to trust in the Lord because He is bigger than us:

"Peace I leave with you; my peace I give to you. **Not as the world gives do I give to you.** Let not your hearts be troubled, neither let them be afraid." John 14:27 (ESV)

"Behold, God is my salvation; I will trust, and will not be afraid; for the Lord God is my strength and my song, **and he has become my salvation**." Isaiah 12:2 (ESV)

"So we can confidently say, 'The Lord is my helper; I will not fear; **what can man do to me?**'" Hebrews 13:6 (ESV)

CHAPTER 4

HAMSTER-ON-WHEEL SYNDROME

Sometimes life responsibilities have us feeling like a hamster on a wheel, running and running but never getting anywhere. It's an unrelenting race that only has one end: Burn-out. Who will help us or step in to give us a break? Jesus says,

> "Come to me, all who labor and are heavy laden, and I will give you rest. Take my yoke upon you, and learn from me, for I am gentle and lowly in heart, and you will find rest for your souls. For my yoke is easy, and my burden is light."
> Matthew 11:28-30 (ESV)

DID YOU KNOW?

What is a YOKE? It's not the yellow thing inside of an egg! A yoke is a double harness which attaches to a cart or plow, used by a pair of oxen or other draft animals to help alleviate the work of hauling. To prevent pain or discomfort, a yoke was hand-carved from wood to fit the neck and shoulders of the animals. In Biblical times, the word yoke was also used as a mark of servitude and submission, as well as for carrying the burden of a task or mission.[1]

Rest For Your Soul

You do not have to carry the weight of life's responsibilities and burdens on your own. Jesus offers us a chance to learn from Him by sharing His yoke with us, like the seasoned ox that guides the young and alleviates the burden of the work load. We are also offered companionship in our labor together, as well as the peace and assurance that if we submit to Christ, our yoke of oppression from slavery to sin will be broken.[2]

"It is for freedom that Christ has set us free. Stand firm, then, and do not let yourselves be burdened again by a yoke of slavery." Galatians 5:1 (NIV)

Ox Training

Two oxen are chosen to share a yoke.

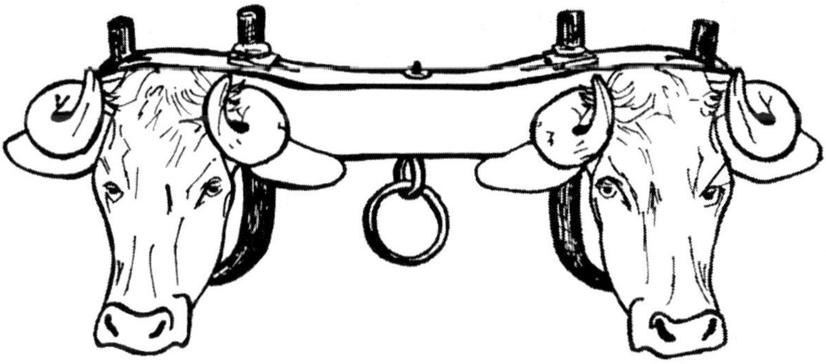

Yoked Oxen / © Jade Creighton

Older, seasoned ox
-Trained and hardy from years of routine
-Leads; draws harder; bears majority of load

Younger, new ox
-Has potential; inexperienced
-Learns from mentor; gains skills/knowledge to train others

By sharing the same yoke with a veteran workhorse, the elder trains the young.[3]

You Will Have Struggles

Does submitting to the yoke of Jesus mean that we will no longer have struggles? No. In fact, the Bible says that in this world, we *will* have struggles – but thankfully, Jesus has overcome this world:

"I have said these things to you, that in me you may have peace. **In the world you will have tribulation. But take heart; I have overcome the world.**" John 16:33 (ESV)

"They preached the good news to that city and made many disciples, then they returned to Lystra and to

Iconium and to Antioch, strengthening and establishing the hearts of the disciples; encouraging them to remain firm in the faith, saying, **'It is through many tribulations and hardships that we must enter the kingdom of God**.'" Acts 14:21-22 (AMP)

"Little children (believers, dear ones), **you are of God and you belong to Him and have [already] overcome them [the agents of the antichrist];** because He who is in you is greater than he (Satan) who is in the world [of sinful mankind]." 1 John 4:4 (AMP)

<u>Do All Things For The Glory Of God, Even The Mundane</u>

My grandmother cooked and cleaned the kitchen for 40 years before my grandfather took up pie making and began to wash dishes. After a little while of cleaning the kitchen on his own, he turned to my grandmother and asked, "How did you stand to wash the same dishes every day for 40 years?"

Sometimes it's easy to labor for the people we want to labor for, or in ways that we enjoy. Then, it's a labor of love. But it's not so easy if we despise the labor or the people we labor for. Then, our labor can feel mundane, unappreciated, or unfair. The cure for this is to do all of our responsibilities for God, **especially the boring and unfair ones.**

"Whatever you do, work at it with all your heart, as working for the Lord, not for human masters, since you know that you will receive an inheritance from the Lord as a reward. It is the Lord Christ you are serving." Colossians 3:23-24 (NIV)

ACTIONABLE INSIGHT

Do all things for the Lord, even things that are mundane or unfair. Whatever your responsibilities, do them lovingly – even if you don't enjoy the work or the people you're working for. Labor instead for an endlessly loving and supportive God.

CHAPTER 5

TITHING WHEN YOU'RE BROKE

What Is Tithing, And Do We Have To Do It?

Have you ever heard that we must give or "tithe" at least ten percent of our income to the church? Hold on… is that before or after taxes?

When I was an atheist, one of the biggest turn-offs about Christianity for me was the passing of the collection plate. I saw church leaders collecting money from their congregations, living lavishly, and then telling people that if they prayed hard enough that they could be rich, too.

What does the Bible have to say about it? According to *Easton's Bible Dictionary,* the dedication of a tenth to God was recognized as a duty before the time of Moses (Genesis 14:20; Hebrews 7:6; Genesis 28:20-22), and the first Old Testament Law of Moses on tithing is recorded in the book of Leviticus.[1]

"A tithe of everything from the land, whether grain from the soil or fruit from the trees, belongs to the LORD; it is holy to the LORD. Whoever would redeem any of their tithe must add a fifth of the value to it. Every tithe of the herd and flock—**every tenth animal that passes under the shepherd's rod** —will be holy to the LORD:" Leviticus 27:30-32 (NIV)

DID YOU KNOW?

The literal translation of tithe = "tenth" or "tenth part" from the Hebrew word *ma'aser.*[2]

Tithing 10%

As Christians, we are no longer under the Old Testament Law of Moses, so tithing a set ten percent is not commanded. We are, however, commanded to give, and to give cheerfully. Jesus advises a rich man to sell **everything** and follow Him (Luke 18:22; Mark 10:21; Matthew 19:21). Each of us should pray and seek God's wisdom on how much to tithe. It matters less about how much we give, and more about giving with an attitude of worship and service to God's Kingdom.

> "When Jesus heard this, He said to him, 'You still lack one thing; sell everything that you have and distribute the money to the poor, and you will have [abundant] treasure in heaven; and come, follow Me [becoming My disciple, believing and trusting in Me and walking the same path of life that I walk].'" Luke 18:22 (AMP)

> "Remember this: Whoever sows sparingly will also reap sparingly, and whoever sows generously will also reap generously. Each of you should give what you have decided in your heart to give, not reluctantly or under compulsion, for God loves a cheerful giver."
> 2 Corinthians 9:6-7 (NIV)

We don't "have to" give ten percent; we could give less. Or, we could give even more. **All of our needs are provided by God, so trusting Him with our finances is an opportunity for us to act on our faith.** It's been said that tithing is not giving, it's returning; which **does not** mean that we will suddenly become wealthy if we donate money to the church. Whatever we give out of obedience to the Lord of our money, our time, or ourselves is being traded in for *heavenly* riches. Jesus instructs us to lay up our treasures in heaven:

> "Do not lay up for yourselves treasures on earth, where moth and rust destroy and where thieves break in and steal, but lay up for yourselves treasures in heaven, where neither moth nor rust destroys and where thieves do not break in and steal. For where your treasure is, there your heart will be also." Matthew 6:19-21 (ESV)

Be Mindful Of Where You Give, But Trust God

As I began to give money to the church, I found out that even regular neighborhood churches are run much like businesses, with bills and salaries to pay. This made me wonder: **If I give to my church, how will my precious, hard-earned money actually be used?**

As with everything, step one is to pray about it. Before you give, pray over your money that it be used rightly. Next, you should give regularly to the church that you attend regularly. If you don't have a church that you attend regularly, or if you don't feel comfortable giving to your church, ask God for guidance as to which church to attend and which ministries to support financially. Avoid "Prosperity Gospel" ministries and churches with questionable financial practices altogether.

Wherever you decide to tithe, trust your church and don't get too hung up on how the church ultimately decides to spend church money. God knows your heart. If you tithe in good faith to a church, and then the church misuses the money – that is between God and the church. **It is our responsibility to give; it is the church's responsibility to use the money wisely and for the greater good of the Kingdom.**

Money Management

Growing up, most of my family and friends didn't have a ton of money. We didn't learn about money management, and most of us shared a common mindset: Clock in somewhere 40+ hours a week, work for The Man, open credit cards, live beyond our means, get student loans, worry about debt later, ignore our credit reports, avoid taking financial risks, don't start our own businesses, scrape together our rent payments, have no retirement plan, work until we're dead, leave our remaining debts to surviving family members.

If this sounds familiar to you, don't fret – you are not alone! I am certainly no expert on finances, but the Lord is. God knows your needs and He will provide for you, because He cannot go back on His Word. Check out what Jesus says in the book of Matthew:

> "Therefore I tell you, **do not be anxious about your life, what you will eat or what you will drink, nor about your body, what you will put on.** Is not life more than

food, and the body more than clothing? Look at the birds of the air: they neither sow nor reap nor gather into barns, and yet your heavenly Father feeds them. Are you not of more value than they? **And which of you by being anxious can add a single hour to his span of life?** And why are you anxious about clothing? Consider the lilies of the field, how they grow: they neither toil nor spin, yet I tell you, even Solomon in all his glory was not arrayed like one of these. But if God so clothes the grass of the field, which today is alive and tomorrow is thrown into the oven, will he not much more clothe you, O you of little faith? **Therefore do not be anxious, saying, 'What shall we eat?' or 'What shall we drink?' or 'What shall we wear?'** For the Gentiles seek after all these things, and **your heavenly Father knows that you need them all. But seek first the kingdom of God and his righteousness, and all these things will be added to you.**"
Matthew 6:25-33 (ESV)

While we might not get the exact provisions that we want, God will give us the exact provisions that we need. That does not mean we can be wasteful or careless, because the scriptures also caution us not to test the Lord (Matthew 4:7).

<u>Enemy Attack/Spiritual Warfare</u>

Have you ever felt like no matter what you do, money runs through your fingers like sand? Sometimes even our finances can fall under enemy attack. Because you are now indwelled with the Holy Spirit and a servant of the God Most High, you have the authority to stand against the devil's schemes in the name of Jesus:

"Put on the full armor of God, so that you can take your stand against the devil's schemes. For our struggle is not against flesh and blood, but against the rulers, against the authorities, against the powers of this dark world and against the spiritual forces of evil in the heavenly realms." Ephesians 6:11-12 (NIV)

Prayer for finances:

Lord Jesus, I come before you and admit that I need You, laying my life down at Your feet. Humble my heart regarding money and take charge of my finances. Place a hedge of protection over my finances and rebuke any attacks of the enemy over my life in the name of Jesus. Lord, all money is Yours. You give and take away as You see fit. I pray for Your will over my life, and for the financial wisdom to use Your money wisely and rightly, in the name of Jesus. All that I have is a gift from You. Thank You for all that You have provided me with and continue to provide me with, in the name of Jesus, Amen.

One of the best things we can do when we're broke or under enemy attack is to thank God for what we do have. Gratitude is a key component to happiness and humility. When we come from a place of gratitude, we have a heightened ability to recognize God's blessings for us in everything.

> "Keep your life free from love of money, and be content with what you have, for he has said, 'I will never leave you nor forsake you.'" Hebrews 13:5 (ESV)

> "Rejoice always, pray continually, give thanks in all circumstances; for this is God's will for you in Christ Jesus." 1 Thessalonians 5:16-18 (NIV)

ACTIONABLE INSIGHT

Thank God with humility and
gratitude for what you DO have.

When I first started going to church, I found out that a lot of people don't tithe. Many of my friends and family members were of the belief that they could not afford to give regularly. They were already struggling financially and had no extra money, so they thought of tithing as just another bill. Most people wanted to support their church, but they talked about tithing like it was some far-off goal that they dreamed of reaching someday. "I will be able to tithe in the future," they'd say. Or, "I'll give later, when I have more money."

Should You Tithe When You're Broke?

Tithing, especially when we're broke, is an opportunity for us to act on our faith – as long as it's done with a cheerful heart, and not begrudgingly or out of obligation. Remember the story of the poor widow's offering?

> "And [Jesus] sat down opposite the treasury and watched the people putting money into the offering box. Many rich people put in large sums. And a poor widow came and put in two small copper coins, which make a penny. And he called his disciples to him and said to them, 'Truly, I say to you, this poor widow has put in more than all those who are contributing to the offering box. For they all contributed out of their abundance, but she out of her poverty has put in everything she had, all she had to live on.'" Mark 12:41-44 (ESV)

Tithe Testimony

I remembered the story of the poor widow one Sunday morning. My bank account balance had dipped under a dollar, and I had about two bucks in my wallet. I took the cash to church that morning and tithed it all. When I checked my account the next day, the balance was equal to about a month's worth of pay due to a random direct-deposit from my old job. Like the poor widow, I gave the most when I had the least, and as a result I was blessed. The Lord gave me the exact provisions that I needed, exactly when I needed them. Tithing will probably not make us rich, but giving regularly (and not just when we have extra money) is an opportunity for us to trust in the Lord's provisions, act on our faith, and lay up our treasures in heaven.

CHAPTER 6

TOXIC MARRIAGE

"But those who marry will face many troubles in this life..." 1 Corinthians 7:28b (NIV)

Even though my spouse and I are both Christians, we have had many heated arguments. Being married is hard. It takes work, time and intention. Couples believe that getting married will fix relationship problems, when in reality marriage puts relationship issues under a microscope. Each of us enters into marriage with a subconscious idea of marital roles and responsibilities, based on our own upbringings and individual "life goggles." Without realizing it, we switch from trying to attract and impress the other person, to trying to change and control the other person, because we want them to fit our vision of what marriage should be. We expect our spouses to know what we think each of our roles and responsibilities are, often without talking to them about it. Then, when our spouses don't meet our expectations, we resent them. It's a vicious cycle of blame, victimization, drama, and pain. The result is a toxic home.

If your marriage has reached this point, you can do a quick heart-check by asking yourself:

Do I still love and care for my spouse?
Do I desire a better marriage relationship?
Is my spouse basically a good person?

And here is the good news: **You can begin to improve your marriage right now, without your spouse having to do anything.** It starts with you. There is hope for your marriage, because Jesus is hope. All you have to do is step aside and allow yourself to rely on Him, which means that you must be willing to look beyond your spouse, and even yourself.

THE HARD FACTS

Stop Making Your Spouse An Idol

Unknowingly and unintentionally, we turn our spouses into idols by making them responsible for our feelings, happiness and sense of self-worth. The only real measure of our worth is that of an unconditionally loving God (*See Chapter 9, Self-Esteem*). Once we recognize this, we can begin to switch our focus from our spouses and ourselves over to God and the bigger picture.

So, like me, suppose you suddenly realize that you've been making your spouse an idol. What can you do about it?

1. **Find your own sense of self-worth through Christ, rather than giving that power to your spouse.**

Do you know who you are in Christ? The Bible tells us exactly what our identity and inheritance is in Christ Jesus (*See Chapter 9, Self-Esteem*). **You were not created for your spouse.** You were not even created for yourself. You were created for God, by God. What are God's assignments for you? What are your God-given talents and spiritual gifts? What things do you enjoy doing, or are naturally good at? How can you use these things to serve and honor the Lord? Ask Him!

2. **Welcome the opportunity to take responsibility for your feelings and behavior.**

We all know that we are solely responsible for our own feelings, and how those feelings cause us to behave – even if we don't want to admit it. The scriptures say that it's ok to feel angry, but that it's not ok to act out in anger:

> "Be angry and do not sin; do not let the sun go down on your anger, and give no opportunity to the devil." Ephesians 4:26-27 (ESV)

No one can *make* us feel or behave a certain way. We all have past traumas, hot buttons, and situations or people that anger us. It's up to us to decide how we are going to feel and react. If we want to be more mature and feel more at peace, then we have to practice controlling our flesh, AKA our behavior. This is a real challenge, and it's often easier said than done. An interesting paradigm: I've failed at controlling my behavior a lot; therefore I've had a lot of practice at it; therefore I'm getting better at it. **Welcome your failures, because they are great practice.**

3. **Make it your job to feel good, which in turn takes the pressure off of your spouse.**

Take a minute to figure out how you really feel. Telling your spouse you feel hurt sounds the same to them as saying, "You hurt me." It doesn't express your actual emotions, and it places blame for your feelings onto them. Telling your spouse that you feel sad, on the other hand, does not blame anybody. Our spouses may hurt us, but they cannot "sad" us. We might feel ignored, belittled or disrespected, but those are just fancy ways of accusing our spouses of ignoring us, belittling us, or disrespecting us. Maybe they are doing those things, but how we really feel is helpless, lonely or scared. When we stop making our spouses idols, we can begin to feel good outside of them, no matter what they are doing (or not doing).

ACTIONABLE INSIGHT

We can rely on Jesus alone for our happiness and contentment. Practice being intentional with your thoughts. Pay attention to what you think, feel and believe (about yourself, your spouse, life, anything). Does it line up with the Bible?

Grass Is Greener Syndrome

Oftentimes we believe that our marital issues are our spouse's fault, and that in order to have a good marriage, we need a new spouse. That is not typically the case. We tend to bring our personal issues with us from relationship to relationship, which is why statistically the divorce rate increases with each subsequent marriage. I read a funny meme the other day: "The grass looks greener on the other side of the fence because you're not over there screwing it up." Instead of trying to fix our spouses, we can improve our relationships immediately as we begin to fix our eyes upon Jesus. **The best thing you can do for yourself and for your marriage is to work on your relationship with the Lord.** And try to make it work with your spouse, because the grass is not greener.

> "May your fountain be blessed, and may you rejoice in the wife of your youth." Proverbs 5:18 (NIV)

Divorce

Have you or your spouse threatened, discussed, or thought about getting a divorce? It is important for your spouse to know that you will not divorce them. That doesn't mean you are now a prisoner to your spouse, or that you can't be apart for a period of time for the purpose of reconciliation. But when the idea of divorce is off the table, then our only option is to figure out solutions. When we persevere through our challenges, we find that we can do things we didn't even realize we were capable of. The Lord uses marriage to grow and mature us, and if we don't take that opportunity with our spouses right now, then we will most likely have the same types of issues come up in our next relationship, and the one after that. **A wise person once shared the secret to a lasting marriage: Don't end it.**

> "For I hate divorce," says the LORD, the God of Israel, "and him who covers his garment with wrong and violence," says the LORD of hosts. "Therefore keep watch on your spirit, so that you do not deal treacherously [with your wife]." Malachi 2:16 (AMP)

DID YOU KNOW?
God hates divorce.
(Malachi 2:26)

What If You Are Already Divorced?

These principals apply to your current marriage relationship, regardless of whether you've been divorced before. Some studies show that the divorce rate in the United States is the same for Christians as it is for non-Christians. There are people who have married and divorced outside of Christ and the church. There are people who have married under Christ and then divorced, even multiple times; some for Biblical reasons, some not. There are even people who have gotten divorced and then remarried – to each other. Whatever your past, our God is a forgiving God:

"Do not judge, and you will not be judged. Do not condemn, and you will not be condemned. Forgive, and you will be forgiven." Luke 6:37 (NIV)

"And when you stand praying, if you hold anything against anyone, forgive them, so that your Father in heaven may forgive you your sins." Mark 11:25 (NIV)

"If we confess our sins, he is faithful and just to forgive us our sins and to cleanse us from all unrighteousness."
1 John 1:9 (ESV)

Turning The Other Cheek

My marriage went through a rocky season where my spouse and I did not want to be around each other. I remember feeling hopeless, lonely, angry, and afraid. In my saddest, most desperate moments, I prayed and cried out to the Lord: "Do you see this, Lord? It's not fair!"

Then the Lord taught me the definition of turning the other cheek. Jesus says,

"If anyone slaps you on the right cheek, turn to them the other cheek also." Matthew 5:39 (NIV)

Surely, turning the other cheek cannot mean that we should lie down and be doormats, or allow others to abuse us. So what exactly does it mean? Let's look at the Amplified Bible:

"You have heard that it was said, 'AN EYE FOR AN EYE, AND A TOOTH FOR A TOOTH [punishment that fits the offense].' But I say to you, **do not resist an evil person [who insults you or violates your rights];** but whoever slaps you on the right cheek, turn the other toward him also **[simply ignore insignificant insults or trivial losses**

and do not bother to retaliate—maintain your dignity, your self-respect, your poise]." Matthew 5:38-39 (AMP)

If your spouse insults you, ignores you, threatens you, calls you names, breaks your trust, or whatever wrong it is that they are doing to you – **it does not give you the right to act out, even in defense of your own boundaries!** (*See Chapter 7, Fighting &Arguing.*)

If you're like me, maybe you have felt like you have to *fight* for justice and righteousness, or that you have to *fight* for yourself and your boundaries – but you don't. The Lord goes before you and fights your battles. **You no longer have to try to accomplish on your own what God has already promised in the Bible.** I always thought that if I was wronged, then my angry reactions were warranted. I thought I had a good reason (and therefore a right) to yell, cry, or storm around irritably. Not only that, but I also thought that it was my husband's job to notice my bad moods and to fix them. This is where Ephesians 4:26, "Be angry and do not sin," comes into play. By fighting and trying to get our spouses to react or behave a certain way, we are unintentionally taking vengeance into our own hands and disobeying the Lord:

"Beloved, never avenge yourselves, but leave it to the wrath of God, for it is written, 'Vengeance is mine, I will repay, says the Lord.' To the contrary, 'if your enemy is hungry, feed him; if he is thirsty, give him something to drink; for by so doing you will heap burning coals on his head.' Do not be overcome by evil, but overcome evil with good." Romans 12:19-21 (ESV)

DID YOU KNOW?
We can uphold justice, righteousness, and boundaries without fighting, because God fights our battles for us. (Ex. 14:14; Deut. 3:22; Deut. 20:4; Josh. 23:10)

<u>God's Promises</u>

God's promises apply to you, and if your spouse is saved, then those promises apply to your spouse as well. It's your job to abide in the Lord, just as it is your spouse's job to abide in the Lord. Whatever wrong your spouse does is between your spouse and God – not between you and your spouse. Likewise, whatever wrong you do is between you and God.

Work on your own responsibilities to God, pray, and allow the Lord to work on your spouse. You are not your spouse's god, just as your spouse is not your god, so you may as well stop trying to force each other to do anything.

> "The LORD will fight for you while you [only need to] **keep silent** and **remain calm**." Exodus 14:14 (AMP)

What If Your Spouse Is Unsaved?

There are Biblical reasons for divorce, but being married to someone who isn't saved is not one of them. If you are married to someone who is unsaved, you have the opportunity to pray for them, lead by example, and allow them to witness how Jesus is working in your life. As Paul writes in one of his letters to the Corinthians,

> "For how do you know, wife, whether you will save your husband [by leading him to Christ]? Or how do you know, husband, whether you will save your wife [by leading her to Christ]?" 1 Corinthians 7:16 (AMP)

Breaking Day

The situation you are in might not be fair, but you can still decide to put God and your spouse first while maintaining good behaviors and boundaries for yourself. Here's how it works: By not treating your spouse poorly, you put your spouse first; by not treating your spouse poorly, you put God first. You can even maintain your own boundaries without treating your spouse poorly. Your spouse might be the worst person that ever lived, but you are abiding in the Lord when you treat them with lovingkindness anyways. Now that you are indwelled with the Holy Spirit, you have the supernatural ability to overcome all things through Christ Jesus.

The root of many arguments is control. When two people become married, each of them begins trying to establish control within the relationship – oftentimes without even realizing it. When communication is great, control and responsibilities are established in a healthy way; but when it's not, even the littlest things can cause huge arguments. That's why it's true what they say: You have to pick your battles.

What If You Are In An Abusive Relationship?

If you are in an abusive or dangerous situation, seek help – especially if your safety or the safety of others is at risk. These situations are often delicate, so you may need to proceed lightly. You may have to go outside of your comfort zone or remove yourself from the situation. Pray and ask God for guidance, courage and protection. We all need to lean on our brothers and sisters; there is no shame in asking for help.

You Are Not Alone

As lonely as we may feel, and as much as we may believe that we have no one, we are never truly alone. When I was an atheist, I had a hard time handling tough situations for two main reasons: I didn't have the Lord to lean on, and I didn't understand my own worth. I had a constant, underlying feeling of loneliness, emptiness, and sadness. If this sounds familiar, keep hanging on. The Lord is with us always. **Our saddest, most desperate moments often lead to our closest, most intimate times with the Lord.** In times of utter loneliness, when we have to lean on the Lord the most, is when He strengthens us to persevere:

> "But he said to me, **'My grace is sufficient for you, for my power is made perfect in weakness.'** Therefore I will boast all the more gladly about my weaknesses, so that Christ's power may rest on me. That is why, for Christ's sake, I delight in weaknesses, in insults, in hardships, in persecutions, in difficulties. For when I am weak, then I am strong." 2 Corinthians 12:9-10 (NIV)

Whatever the situation, we can get through it knowing that we are children of the God Most High. We now have a roaring lion – Jesus Christ – by our side. He will go before us and fight our battles for us; all we have to do is let Him.

CHAPTER 7

FIGHTING & ARGUING

Did you grow up in a household where fighting and arguing were normalized? Maybe the only way to be heard was to use bad language or to yell the loudest. Maybe the only way to defend yourself or your property was to fight. Maybe this is how you're living right now. Remember what Jesus says in the book of Matthew?

> "But I say to you, do not resist an evil person [who insults you or violates your rights]; but whoever slaps you on the right cheek, turn the other toward him also [simply ignore insignificant insults or trivial losses and do not bother to retaliate—maintain your dignity, your self-respect, your poise]." Matthew 5:39 (AMP)

What does it mean to "simply ignore insignificant insults or trivial losses"? Surely, it can't mean that we should bottle up our emotions or sweep our problems under the rug. So then, which insults and losses are considered trivial and insignificant, and which aren't? What if the insults are significant and the losses are substantial? And most importantly – who gets to decide?

Looking Through The Scope Of Eternity

> "Therefore we do not lose heart. Though outwardly we are wasting away, yet inwardly we are being renewed day by day. **For our light and momentary troubles are achieving for us an eternal glory that far outweighs them all.** So we fix our eyes not on what is seen, but on what is unseen, **since what is seen is temporary, but what is unseen is eternal**." 2 Corinthians 4:16-18 (NIV)

Paul describes the troubles of this life as *light* and *momentary*. Think about eternity, and what you might be doing when you get there. Are the things you are fighting and arguing about relevant in the scope of eternity? Think of eternity as a pie chart, where our earthly lives are a barely visible sliver. Imagine eternal glory. Is it even possible for the people and situations that are bothering us today to be relevant *in the scope of eternity*?

DID YOU KNOW?

We only live temporarily, but this life is just the beginning. What's in store for us next is an eternity in heaven with Christ. (John 3:16; Rom. 6:23; John 6:40)

> "And God will wipe away every tear from their eyes; there shall be no more death, nor sorrow, nor crying. There shall be no more pain, for the former things have passed away." Revelation 21:4 (NKJV)

Once we are in heaven for eternity, our trials and tribulations come to an end; **therefore, in the scope of eternity, all insults are insignificant and all losses are trivial.**

Of course, that doesn't mean that we should be uncaring or unloving during our time here. We should be passionate and caring as we go through life with one another. Consider what Jesus said when questioned by some of the religious leaders of His time, known as the Pharisees:

> "One of them, an expert in the law, tested him with this question: 'Teacher, which is the greatest commandment in the Law?' Jesus replied: **'Love the Lord your God with all your heart and with all your soul and with all your mind.'** This is the first and greatest commandment. And the second is like it: **'Love your neighbor as yourself.'** All the Law and the Prophets hang on these two commandments." Matthew 22:35-40 (NIV)

We are made and instructed to love. It's one of the ways God displays His goodness through us, making it possible for us to love our families, our friends, and our enemies – even when we don't like them in the moment. Paul gives us this advice in the book of Romans:

> "Bless those who persecute you; bless and do not curse them. Rejoice with those who rejoice, weep with those who weep. Live in harmony with one another. Do not be haughty, but associate with the lowly. Never be wise in your own sight. Repay no one evil for evil, but give thought to do what is honorable in the sight of all. If possible, **so far as it depends on you,** live peaceably with all. Beloved, never avenge yourselves, but leave it to the wrath of God, for it is written, 'Vengeance is mine, I will repay, says the Lord.' To the contrary, 'if your enemy is hungry, feed him; if he is thirsty, give him something to drink; for by so doing you will heap burning coals on his head.' Do not be overcome by evil, but overcome evil with good." Romans 12:14-21 (ESV)

This goes in line with turning the other cheek (Matthew 5:39). When someone wrongs us – though we may be right in our anger about it – we do not have a free pass to behave however we want to, or in ways that are not pleasing to the Lord. It is our job to abide in the Lord and to control our own behavior. All it takes is a little faith, a bit of useful information, and some practice.

<u>God Vs. Satan</u>

God is omnipresent – everywhere, all the time; the devil is not. God runs after us; the devil runs away from us. Our fight is a spiritual battle, but we **do not** suffer through it alone.

DID YOU KNOW?
God is Omnipresent;
Satan is not![1]

> "Submit yourselves therefore to God. Resist the devil, and he will flee from you. Draw near to God, and he will draw near to you." James 4:7-8a (ESV)

> "Resist him, firm in your faith, knowing that the same kinds of suffering are being experienced by your brotherhood throughout the world." 1 Peter 5:9 (ESV)

Fighting Spiritual Battles

How do we fight spiritual battles that are not against flesh and blood? God gives us His very own armor to take stand against the schemes of the devil:

> "Finally, be strong in the Lord and in his mighty power. Put on the full armor of God, so that you can take your stand against the devil's schemes. For our struggle is not against flesh and blood, but against the rulers, against the authorities, against the powers of this dark world and against the spiritual forces of evil in the heavenly realms. Therefore put on the full armor of God, so that when the day of evil comes, you may be able to stand your ground, and after you have done everything, to stand. Stand firm then, with **the belt of truth buckled around your waist**, with **the breastplate of righteousness in place**, and with **your feet fitted with the readiness that comes from the gospel of peace**. In addition to all this, **take up the shield of faith,** with which you can extinguish all the flaming arrows of the evil one. **Take the helmet of salvation and the sword of the Spirit**, which is the word of God. And **pray in the Spirit** on all occasions with all kinds of prayers and requests. With this in mind, be alert and always keep on praying for all the Lord's people." Ephesians 6:10-18 (NIV)

The Armor Of God

Belt of Truth – Core support; protects vital organs; provides backing in the midst of spiritual warfare

Breastplate of Righteousness – Right living

Shoes of Peace – Inner, eternal stability; enables us to live harmoniously with others

Shield of Faith – Application of beliefs

Helmet of Salvation – Blessings; status; identity

Sword of the Spirit – The Word of God

Prayer – Activates armor[2]

What To Do In An Argument

1. Praise God

Praise the Lord in the midst of all hardships, especially during fights and arguments. Right in the middle of an argument, stop and thank the Lord for anything you can think of. Is someone doing something to you that you don't like? Thank God that He would never do that thing to you. Are you being put down or insulted? Thank God for loving you as you are. Think of some descriptive words for God and thank Him for being those things. If you can't think of anything, just speak the name of Jesus.

DID YOU KNOW?
There is power in our praises! Praising God produces supernatural results. The enemy cannot stand to be in the presence of God's praises. (Psalm 8:2)

Thank You God…

…That You would never abandon me
…For loving me as I am
…For being loving, caring, kind, righteous, gracious, forgiving, almighty
…For the breath in my lungs
…Thank You Jesus

2. Walk away and pray

If you are in an argument, or if you can sense that an argument is brewing, walk away. Go to another room, go for a walk or a drive, and spend some time alone praying and venting to God about what's bothering you. Be patient while you wait on the Lord. While He may not change the people or situations that are challenging for you, He can change *you.* Some of our most challenging situations are used to refine and mature us, while also showing us how to rely on the Lord.

Sometimes the Lord allows the heat to be turned up in order to bring our impurities to the surface, so that they may be sloughed off.

> "The refining pot is for silver and the furnace for gold, But the LORD tests hearts." Proverbs 17:3 (AMP)

> "The beginning of strife is like letting out water, so quit before the quarrel breaks out." Proverbs 17:14 (ESV)

Act On Your Faith (Strife Prevention)

One of the most difficult things for me to do as a former atheist is to act on my faith. It can feel weird, counter-intuitive, unnatural, or even embarrassing; but we must **believe** in our hearts and souls that God's Word is the **truth**, no matter how we **feel**. We can act on our faith to make our homes feel more peaceful and to help prevent future fights from breaking out:

1. Protect Your Eye Gates and Your Ear Gates

Protecting our eye gates and ear gates means being intentional about what we allow into our line of vision and hearing, by being selective about the content we choose to intake. This includes everything from the movies we choose to watch, to the music we choose to listen to, and even the words we choose to speak. Sometimes we are exposed to things that we do not want to see or hear, especially if we live with other people, and so we can't always protect our eye gates and ear gates. If your home has been exposed to bad content, including fighting and arguing, you can "air it out" with prayer and refill it with the Word of God.

2. Cleanse Your Home with Prayer

Be specific with your prayers. Pray out loud by name against divorce, strife, arguing, fighting, name-calling, sickness, nightmares, or whatever is going on in your home. If you have blessed oil, you can use it in your home as you pray:

As for me and my house, we shall serve the Lord! This home belongs to You, Lord; You are welcome here. Lord Jesus, I rebuke the plans and the schemes of the enemy over my family and over my home in Your Mighty Name. The enemy is not welcome here! Divorce is not welcome here; strife is not welcome here; arguing is not welcome here; fighting is not welcome here; name-calling is not welcome here; sickness is not welcome here; nightmares are not welcome here. Lord, I pray for Your supernatural peace and joy to dwell in this place. May this home be a suitable resting place for You and Your heavenly angels. In Jesus' name, Amen!

3. Refill Your Home with the Word of God

Once your house is cleansed, don't leave it empty! Fill it up with God's spoken Word:

-Read your Bible out loud
-Play YouTube videos of scripture being read
-Listen to worship/Christian music

Questions To Consider:

Would you be ashamed to invite Jesus into your home? Why? What needs to change?

CHAPTER 8

QUITTING

Bad habits are hard to break. Addictions seem impossible to overcome. We can't seem to quit them on our own – but with God, all things are possible:

> "But Jesus looked at them and said, 'With man this is impossible, but with God all things are possible.'" Matthew 19:26 (ESV)

And we know that as born-again believers in Christ, we have been made new because of the indwelling of the Holy Spirit:

> "So from now on we regard no one from a human point of view [according to worldly standards and values]. Though we have known Christ from a human point of view, now we no longer know Him in this way. **Therefore if anyone is in Christ [that is, grafted in, joined to Him by faith in Him as Savior], he is a new creature [reborn and renewed by the Holy Spirit]; the old things [the previous moral and spiritual condition] have passed away.** Behold, new things have come [because spiritual awakening brings a new life]."
> 2 Corinthians 5:16-17 (AMP)

That doesn't necessarily mean that our bad habits and addictions are magically gone. **You are a work in progress.** God already knows you need Him. Plenty of people have been miraculously delivered from addiction, **but sometimes changing our bad habits is a gradual refining process, where we fail and try again over time.**

"The refining pot is for silver and the furnace for gold, But the LORD tests hearts." Proverbs 17:3 (AMP)

"And we know that all things work together for good to those who love God, to those who are the called according to His purpose." Romans 8:28 (NKJV)

That means **God uses hardships in order to make us better, for our own good and for His glory**. He turns up the heat in order to purify us, like the furnace for gold. Have you struggled with your fair share of bad habits and addictions? Some of them may be easy to let go of, while others we cling to and struggle with daily.

Maybe you feel like Paul in Romans 7: You want to do good but you keep going back to your old ways, and it feels like you have to unlearn all of the bad habits that you have learned your whole life.

"For I know that good itself does not dwell in me, that is, in my sinful nature. For I have the desire to do what is good, but I cannot carry it out. For I do not do the good I want to do, but the evil I do not want to do—this I keep on doing. Now if I do what I do not want to do, it is no longer I who do it, but it is sin living in me that does it." Romans 7:18-20 (NIV)

Everyone sins, even revered Bible heroes like Paul. It's normal to have bad days and revert back to our old ways. If we didn't have bad days, how could we truly appreciate the good ones? I still mess up a lot because I often don't take my own advice, even though I know it works. Practice. Mess up. Be embarrassed.

The Bible says that if we resist the devil, he will flee from us (James 4:7), which means that when we overcome our temptations, the devil will leave us alone. The Bible also says that God will not allow us to be tempted beyond what we can bear, and that He will provide a way out for us:

"No temptation has overtaken you except what is common to mankind. And God is faithful; he will not let you be tempted beyond what you can bear. But when you are tempted, he will also provide a way out so that you can endure it." 1 Corinthians 10:13 (NIV)

In addition to resisting the devil, when we draw near to God, God draws near to us (James 4:8). Resist the devil, draw near to the Lord, and take comfort in knowing that He will not allow temptations beyond what you can handle.

ACTIONABLE INSIGHT

Allow yourself to keep learning and growing, and don't be too hard on yourself during the refining process.

Everything In Moderation

Do you smoke once a year at a party? Or do you smoke a pack a day. Do you have a beer or two on the weekend? Or do you have a case every night. Do you eat a scoop of ice cream after dinner? Or do you eat the whole carton.

The Bible tells us not to be gluttonous, not to get drunk, and not to be an adulterer. It doesn't say 'never eat,' 'never drink,' or 'never have sex'. It's just that now, as children of Christ, we strive to do these things with self-control in a respectable way that is pleasing to the Lord.

"**But I say, walk by the Spirit, and you will not gratify the desires of the flesh.** For the desires of the flesh are against the Spirit, and the desires of the Spirit are against the flesh, for these are opposed to each other, to keep you from doing the things you want to do. But if you are led by the Spirit, you are not under the law. Now the works of the flesh are evident: sexual immorality, impurity, sensuality, idolatry, sorcery, enmity, strife, jealousy, fits of anger, rivalries, dissensions, divisions, envy, drunkenness, orgies, and things like these. I warn you, as I warned you before, that those who do such things will not inherit the kingdom of God. **But the fruit of the**

> **Spirit is love, joy, peace, patience, kindness, goodness, faithfulness, gentleness, self-control; against such things there is no law. And those who belong to Christ Jesus have crucified the flesh with its passions and desires."** Galatians 5:16-24 (ESV)

> "So, whether you eat or drink, or whatever you do, do all to the glory of God." 1 Corinthians 10:31 (ESV)

Take Care Of Your Temple

It's ok to have fun and enjoy life. It's not ok to overdo it. The Holy Spirit lives in you; your body is now His home. He's taken up residence in these old meat bags, so let's give him a nice place to hang out and stay a while.

> "Do you not know that your bodies are temples of the Holy Spirit, who is in you, whom you have received from God? You are not your own; you were bought at a price. Therefore honor God with your bodies."
> 1 Corinthians 6:19-20 (NIV)

Don't Violate Your Own Conscience

If a certain habit, lifestyle choice or addiction is weighing on your heart, examine it and pray about it specifically. Each of us is a unique creation, and we each have our different weaknesses. Pray, ask for prayer, and lean on your brothers and sisters in Christ.

> "But each person is tempted when he is lured and enticed by his own desire." James 1:14 (ESV)

What might be considered sinful for one person doesn't necessarily make it so for the next, so ask the Lord to search your heart and see what comes up for you.

> "One person considers one day more sacred than another; another considers every day alike. Each of them should be fully convinced in their own mind. Whoever regards

one day as special does so to the Lord. Whoever eats meat does so to the Lord, for they give thanks to God; and whoever abstains does so to the Lord and gives thanks to God." Romans 14:5-6 (NIV)

Pray and consider the questions below.

1. What is my bad habit or addiction?
2. Do I really want to quit?
3. If I quit, how would my lifestyle change for the worse?
4. If I quit, how would my lifestyle change for the better?
5. Am I afraid of these changes? Why?

CHAPTER 9

SELF-ESTEEM

What is self-esteem, or self-worth? **Self-esteem is our perception of our own value, measured against our perception of someone else's value.** We place so much importance on other people that we measure our own worth based on what other people think and do. Our own standards are formed by what we see going on in the world, based on what others are doing.

We often have low self-esteem because we compare ourselves to others, even unintentionally, and we feel like we don't measure up. We set standards for ourselves that we could never meet. We care about what certain people think of us. We care about fitting in, when and where we want to fit in, among our own peers, friends and families. We measure our own value based on looks, statuses, labels and diagnoses.

What would it be like to be measured against a different standard – one that has nothing to do with you or other people? What would it feel like to forget what anyone else thinks of you, and to forget even the things that you think about yourself?

Through Christ, we find our value outside of other people, and even outside of ourselves. The only true standard of measure is that of an *unconditionally loving* God. That means God loves us no matter what – even when we don't love ourselves. **No human being is capable of offering us that kind of love.**

Identity In Christ

People might try to define you, set standards for you, and tell you what they think of you – but what does God think about you? By understanding our identity and inheritance in Christ Jesus, we can stand firm in who we are and never be convinced otherwise:

✓ You are a child of God. (John 1:12)
✓ You have peace with God. (Rom. 5:1)
✓ The Holy Spirit lives within you. (1 Cor. 3:16)
✓ You have access to God's wisdom. (Jas. 1:5)
✓ You are helped by God. (Heb. 4:16)
✓ You are reconciled to God. (Rom. 5:11)
✓ You are not condemned by God. (Rom. 8:1)
✓ You are justified. (Rom. 5:1)
✓ You have Christ's righteousness. (Rom. 5:19; 2 Cor. 5:21)
✓ You are completely forgiven. (Col. 1:14)
✓ You are tenderly loved by God. (Jer. 31:3)
✓ You are the sweet fragrance of Christ to God. (2 Cor. 2:15)
✓ You are a temple in which God dwells. (1 Cor. 3:16)
✓ You are blameless beyond reproach. (Col. 1:22)
✓ You are the salt of the earth. (Matt. 5:13)
✓ You are the light of the world. (Matt. 5:14)
✓ You are a branch on Christ's vine. (John 15:1,5)
✓ You are Christ's friend. (John 15:15)
✓ You are chosen by Christ to bear fruit. (John 15:16)
✓ You are a joint heir with Christ, sharing His inheritance with Him. (Rom. 8:17)
✓ You are united to the Lord, one spirit with Him. (1 Cor. 6:17)
✓ You are a member of Christ's body. (1 Cor. 12:27)
✓ You are a saint. (Eph. 1:1)
✓ You are hidden with Christ in God. (Col. 3:3)
✓ You are chosen by God, holy and dearly loved. (Col. 3:12)
✓ You are a child of the light. (1 Thess. 5:5)
✓ You are holy, and you share in God's heavenly calling. (Heb. 3:1)
✓ You are sanctified. (Heb. 2:11)
✓ You are one of God's living stones, being built up in Christ as a spiritual house. (1 Pet. 2:5)
✓ You are a member of a chosen race, a royal priesthood, a holy nation, a people for God's own possession and created to sing His praises. (1 Pet. 2:9-10)
✓ You are firmly rooted and built up in Christ. (Col. 2:7)
✓ You are born of God, and the evil one cannot touch you. (1 John 5:18)
✓ You have the mind of Christ. (1 Cor. 2:16)
✓ You may approach God with boldness, freedom, and confidence. (Eph. 3:12)

- ✓ You have been rescued from Satan's domain and transferred into the kingdom of Christ. (Col. 1:13)
- ✓ You have been made complete in Christ. (Col. 2:10)
- ✓ You have been given a spirit of power, love, and self-discipline. (2 Tim. 1:7)
- ✓ You have been given great and precious promises by God. (2 Pet. 1:4)
- ✓ Your needs are met by God. (Phil. 4:19)
- ✓ You are a prince (or princess) in God's kingdom. (John 1:12; 1 Tim. 6:15)
- ✓ You have been bought with a price, and you belong to God. (1 Cor. 6:19,20)
- ✓ You have been adopted as God's child. (Eph. 1:5)
- ✓ You have direct access to God through the Holy Spirit. (Eph. 2:18)
- ✓ You are assured that all things are working together for good. (Rom. 8:28)
- ✓ You are free from any condemning charges against you. (Rom. 8:31)
- ✓ You cannot be separated from the love of God. (Rom. 8:35)
- ✓ You have been established, anointed, and sealed by God. (2 Cor. 1:21,22)
- ✓ You are confident that the good work that God has begun in you will be perfected. (Phil. 3:20)
- ✓ You are a personal witness of Christ's. (Acts 1:8)
- ✓ You are God's co-worker (2 Cor. 6:1; 1 Cor. 3:9)
- ✓ You are seated with Christ in the heavenly realm. (Eph. 2:6)
- ✓ You are God's workmanship. (Eph. 2:10)
- ✓ You can do all things through Christ, who gives you the strength you need. (Phil. 4:13)

List adapted from Priscilla Shirer's *Armor of God.*[1]

DID YOU KNOW?

You are served by angels! Because we are created in His image and redeemed by Christ, we are highly valued by God. As heirs of salvation, God sends angels to render service and minister to us. (Hebrews 1:14)

"Are not all angels ministering spirits sent to serve those who will inherit salvation?" Hebrews 1:14 (NIV)

Does God Make Mistakes?

Were you born the wrong way? Too early? Too late? The wrong color? The wrong gender? Were you even supposed to be born at all?

Because God is the Author and Creator of all things, He does not and cannot make mistakes. Maybe your earthly parents didn't plan you, or didn't even want you, but your Heavenly Father did. Maybe you believe that you should have been born differently, or not born at all, but God knew you before you were born and stitched you together in the womb. God's Word tells us that we were created by design, with intention, and for a purpose – regardless of what anyone, **including our own selves,** has to say about it.

> "For you formed my inward parts; you knitted me together in my mother's womb. I praise you, for I am fearfully and wonderfully made. Wonderful are your works; my soul knows it very well. My frame was not hidden from you, when I was being made in secret, intricately woven in the depths of the earth. Your eyes saw my unformed substance; in your book were written, every one of them, the days that were formed for me, when as yet there was none of them."
> Psalm 139:13-16 (ESV)

Take time to really think about that. You are an intricate masterpiece formed by the hand of God, the Great Potter and Creator of the Universe. God knew the exact number of our days on earth before we were even born.

So it doesn't matter what we look like, how we feel, where we're from, who our parents were (or are), or whatever it is that we may think is wrong with us. **We were created by God for His enjoyment and purposes – not for our own or anyone else's.** That means He made you just the way He wanted to, on purpose, for His glory and for your good; to build your character and to draw your heart nearer to Him – and He loves you right where you are.

Take Your Thoughts Captive

> "We destroy arguments and every lofty opinion raised against the knowledge of God, **and take every thought captive to obey Christ,"** 2 Corinthians 10:5 (ESV)

Sometimes our own negative thoughts can be our worst enemy, but with a little practice it is possible to retrain our brains and stop negative thinking patterns. The first step is awareness: Once we realize we are in a negative thinking pattern, we can recognize it and put a stop to it. Whenever I catch myself thinking negatively, I pray in the name of Jesus and say the word STOP in my mind. It helps me to think of this scripture:

DID YOU KNOW?

FACTS ABOUT THE DEVIL

Creator of Nothing:
-Only perverts what God has created (Acts 13:10)

Fallen Angel:
-Has no chance for redemption (Luke 10:18)

Does Not Love:
-Seeks to prevent our salvation (Luke 8:12)

Father of Lies:
-There is no truth in him (John 8:44)

> "Finally, brothers and sisters, whatever is **true**, whatever is **noble**, whatever is **right**, whatever is **pure**, whatever is **lovely**, whatever is **admirable**—if anything is **excellent** or **praiseworthy**—think about such things... **And the God of Peace will be with you."** Philippians 4:8,9b (NIV)

I tell this scripture to my little daughter when she has a bad dream. We even posted it on her bedroom wall so she can read it before bed. When I focus my attention on remembering all of the things in this scripture, I get distracted away from my negative thoughts. I made a little series of pictures to help my daughter and me to remember:

True Noble Right Pure Lovely Admirable Excellent Praise-worthy

Philippians 4:8 / © Jade Creighton

DID YOU KNOW?
Jesus was described as having no beauty and an undesirable physical appearance. (Isaiah 53:2)

Worldly Beauty

If you are familiar with pain and suffering, and if you are despised, rejected, and unattractive to the world, then you are in good company:

"He had no beauty or majesty to attract us to him, nothing in his appearance that we should desire him. He was despised and rejected by mankind, a man of suffering, and familiar with pain. Like one from whom people hide their faces he was despised, and we held him in low esteem." Isaiah 53:2b-3 (NIV)

"But our citizenship is in heaven, and from it we await a Savior, the Lord Jesus Christ, who will transform our lowly body to be like his glorious body, by the power that enables him even to subject all things to himself." Philippians 3:20-21 (ESV)

DID YOU KNOW?
We will get a new body in heaven, free of flaws and ailments. (Phil. 3:21)

We know that we will be given an unflawed body in heaven, but for now we have to make do with what we've got – so let's start loving ourselves like God loves us, existing in the truth of who we are in Christ, and measuring our worth against the only true standard: the Bible.

CHAPTER 10

FEAR OF GOD

Fear God? Wait a minute – isn't God supposed to be loving and kind?

As an atheist, the concept of fearing God made no sense to me. Why would anyone want to worship an angry old sky-man? As a Christian, I especially didn't understand the concept of fearing God. Isn't God love? Isn't God caring? Aren't we His precious children?

The fear of God is not the same thing as being *afraid* of God. He is not a monster or an enraged old man who waits in the sky ready to punish us. God *is* love, God *is* caring, and we *are* His precious children – and because He loves us, He corrects and disciplines us like good and wise parents do. When my little daughter used to run towards the street oblivious to oncoming traffic, I would yell at her and even threaten to spank her. That's because I love her and care about her safety. I had to discipline and correct her until she was mature enough to understand that the street can be dangerous, and the importance of looking both ways before crossing.

> "As a father shows compassion to his children, so the Lord shows compassion to those who fear him."
> Psalm 103:13 (ESV)

In the same sense, as sons and daughters of God, we will be disciplined by God. It is an indicator that we are His children:

> "Endure hardship as discipline; God is treating you as his children. For what children are not disciplined by their father? **If you are not disciplined—and everyone undergoes discipline—then you are not legitimate, not true sons and daughters at all.** Moreover, we have all

had human fathers who disciplined us and we respected them for it. How much more should we submit to the Father of spirits and live! They disciplined us for a little while as they thought best; **but God disciplines us for our good, in order that we may share in his holiness.** No discipline seems pleasant at the time, but painful. Later on, however, it produces a harvest of righteousness and peace for those who have been trained by it."
Hebrews 12:7-11 (NIV)

"My son, do not despise the Lord's discipline, and do not resent his rebuke, because the Lord disciplines those he loves, as a father the son he delights in."
Proverbs 3:11-12 (NIV)

What Kind Of Dad Did You Have?

Some people were raised by unkind or unloving fathers; others didn't have a father at all. I've heard an interesting concept that our fear of God may mirror the fear we have of our earthly fathers. For example, if you were afraid of getting in trouble with your tough, disciplinarian dad, you might view God as a tough disciplinarian and be afraid of His discipline. If you had no father, you may feel like God has abandoned you. While the 'dad' concept may or may not be true, what matters is being conscious of our own, personal view of God. Are we measuring Him against our preconceived notions of authority figures, based on our own life experiences? Or are we measuring God against the one true standard, His written Word?

Best Father In The Universe

If you struggle in your relationship with your earthly father or mother, or if you don't have earthly parents, remember: You are now an adopted child of the God Most High. **There are no orphans in the Kingdom of God…**

"Yet to all who did receive him, to those who believed in his name, he gave the right to become children of God—children born not of natural descent, nor of human decision or a husband's will, but born of God." John 1:12-13 (NIV)

"For you did not receive the spirit of slavery to fall back into fear, but you have received the Spirit of adoption as sons, by whom we cry, 'Abba! Father!' The Spirit himself bears witness with our spirit that we are children of God, and if children, then heirs—heirs of God and fellow heirs with Christ, provided we suffer with him in order that we may also be glorified with him." Romans 8:15-17 (ESV)

...And your Heavenly Father is rich.

"For he chose us in him before the creation of the world to be holy and blameless in his sight. **In love he predestined us for adoption to sonship through Jesus Christ,** in accordance with his pleasure and will— to the praise of his glorious grace, which he has freely given us in the One he loves. **In him we have redemption through his blood, the forgiveness of sins, in accordance with the riches of God's grace that he lavished on us.** With all wisdom and understanding, he made known to us the mystery of his will according to his good pleasure, which he purposed in Christ, to be put into effect when the times reach their fulfillment—to bring unity to all things in heaven and on earth under Christ. **In him we were also chosen, having been predestined according to the plan of him who works out everything in conformity with the purpose of his will,** in order that we, who were the first to put our hope in Christ, might be for the praise of his glory. **And you also were included in Christ when you heard the message of truth, the gospel of your salvation.** When you believed, **you were marked in him with a seal, the promised Holy Spirit, who is a deposit guaranteeing our inheritance** until the redemption of those who are God's possession—to the praise of his glory."Ephesians 1:4-14 (NIV)

Do You Fear The Lord?

If fearing God does not mean being afraid of God – what does it mean? Fearing God means standing in awe of Him, respecting Him, obeying Him, submitting to His discipline, humbling ourselves before Him, and having an exalted, reverential view of Him which greatly impacts the way we live.[1] The opposite of standing in awe of God and fearing Him is having a hardened and unreceptive heart.

> "Let all the earth **fear the LORD**; Let all the inhabitants of the world **stand in awe of Him.**" Psalm 33:8 (NKJV)

> "These are the ones I look on with favor: those who are **humble and contrite in spirit, and who tremble at my word.**" Isaiah 66:2b (NIV)

> "Blessed is the one who **always trembles** before God, but whoever **hardens their heart** falls into trouble."
> Proverbs 28:14 (NIV)

> "**The fear of the LORD is the beginning of knowledge;** fools despise wisdom and instruction."
> Proverbs 1:7 (ESV)

> "… continue to work out your salvation [that is, cultivate it, bring it to full effect, actively pursue spiritual maturity] **with awe-inspired fear and trembling** [using serious caution and critical self-evaluation to avoid anything that might offend God or discredit the name of Christ]."
> Philippians 2:12 (AMP)

What does it mean to tremble before God? One way is similar to being star-struck, but times infinity. Have you ever met your favorite celebrity? Imagine meeting the Creator of the Universe. Not only did God create our favorite athletes, musicians, and artists; He created the human body, music, and art itself. The giftings of our favorite celebrities only further puts God's awesomeness on display. If we can become star-struck over people, how much more would we tremble before the Creator of *Everything*? We cannot even look upon God's face and live.

> "'But,' he said, 'you cannot see my face, **for no one may see me and live.**'"Exodus 33:20 (NIV)

There is also a different kind of fear and trembling in Christ. It is the fear of God's wrath. **God's grace in Christ is our safety from God's wrath outside of Christ.** Outside of Christ, there is absolute terror.[2]

> "And do not fear those who kill the body but cannot kill the soul. Rather fear him who can destroy both soul and body in hell." Matthew 10:28 (ESV)

As an atheist, I didn't believe in an afterlife. Pop-culture depicts hell as a fun place where bad boys get to go to keep having fun after they die. There is no mention of what heaven and hell are really like. As a Christian, the last place I want to be is hell. I want to be in the presence of the Lord for all eternity. I want to hear, "Well done, good and faithful servant." I am **afraid** of hearing, "Depart from me, I never knew you."

> "His master replied, 'Well done, good and faithful servant! You have been faithful with a few things; I will put you in charge of many things. Come and share your master's happiness!'" Matthew 25:21 (NIV), *The Parable of Talents*

> "Not everyone who says to me, 'Lord, Lord,' will enter the kingdom of heaven, **but the one who does the will of my Father who is in heaven.** On that day many will say to me, 'Lord, Lord, did we not prophesy in your name, and cast out demons in your name, **and do many mighty works in your name?'** And then will I declare to them, **'I never knew you; depart from me, you workers of lawlessness.'**" Matthew 7:21-23 (ESV), from Jesus' *Sermon on the Mount*

But we cannot earn or work our way into heaven. Our works are "like filthy rags" (Isaiah 64:6) because God graciously gives us the free gift of salvation through faith. Salvation is not something we can earn, and good works cannot be done on our own. We were created by God to do good works through Christ:

"For it is by grace you have been saved, through faith—and this is not from yourselves, it is the gift of God— not by works, so that no one can boast. For we are God's handiwork, **created in Christ Jesus to do good works, which God prepared in advance for us to do**."
Ephesians 2:8-10 (NIV)

CHAPTER 11

HEALING

Human anatomy is some of God's finest handiwork. The intricacy of how our bodies function on every level is a living miracle. Some of mankind's greatest inventions are mere copies of God's various designs throughout our bodies. This is no accident. Our bodies were created by God on purpose, by design, with care and intention. If God created your body, God can heal your body.

We already know from the scriptures that we will get a new body in heaven, free of flaws and ailments:

> "But our citizenship is in heaven, and from it we await a Savior, the Lord Jesus Christ, **who will transform our lowly body to be like his glorious body,** by the power that enables him even to subject all things to himself." Philippians 3:20-21 (ESV)

And we will also be free of mental anguish:

> "And God will wipe away every tear from their eyes; there shall be no more death, nor sorrow, nor crying. There shall be no more pain, for the former things have passed away." Revelation 21:4 (NKJV)

But what about today, in this life, here on earth? Like with our finances or anything else, just because we pray for something does not mean we will get it, so healing in this life is NOT a guarantee – but why not? Does God want us to be sick?

Where Does Illness Come From?

Time and again throughout the Bible, Jesus heals, removes sickness, casts out demons, and raises people from the dead. Never does He make a person sick, put a demon in someone, or kill anyone. Illness is not of Christ; therefore, illness is not of God. Let's look at what Paul, who penned the majority of the New Testament, writes about his own ailment:

> "So to keep me from becoming conceited because of the surpassing greatness of the revelations, **a thorn was given me in the flesh, a messenger of Satan to harass me, to keep me from becoming conceited**."
> 2 Corinthians 12:7 (ESV)

Paul says that his 'thorn in the flesh' came from a messenger of Satan. Just as God allowed the devil to torment Job (read the book of Job in the Old Testament), God allowed the devil to torment Paul for Paul's own good and for God's own glory. This is Paul's advice regarding a sexually immoral man:

> "...deliver such a one to Satan for the destruction of the flesh, that his spirit may be saved in the day of the Lord Jesus." 1 Corinthians 5:5 (NKJV)

Paul's advice is similar to the advice which Jesus repeats on two separate occasions in the book of Matthew:

> "If your right eye makes you stumble and leads you to sin, tear it out and throw it away [that is, remove yourself from the source of temptation]; for it is better for you to lose one of the parts of your body, than for your whole body to be thrown into hell. If your right hand makes you stumble and leads you to sin, cut it off and throw it away [that is, remove yourself from the source of temptation]; for it is better for you to lose one of the parts of your body than for your whole body to go into hell."
> Matthew 5:29-30 (AMP)

"If your hand or your foot causes you to stumble and sin, cut it off and throw it away from you [that is, remove yourself from the source of temptation]; it is better for you to enter life crippled or lame, than to have two hands or two feet and be thrown into everlasting fire. If your eye causes you to stumble and sin, pluck it out and throw it away from you [that is, remove yourself from the source of temptation]; it is better for you to enter life with only one eye, than to have two eyes and be thrown into the fiery hell." Matthew 18:8-9 (AMP)

This is part of our refining process. While sickness, illness, disease, and ailment are all attacks of the enemy, they can be used for God's good purposes to mature, grow, and refine us in Christ, while also directing our path in regard to the bigger picture. God knows the plans He has for us; we have only to trust Him.

DID YOU KNOW?
Our sinful flesh can be destroyed – by Satan – for our good and for God's glory. (1 Cor. 5:5)

"And we know that **all things** work together for good to those who love God, to those who are the called according to His purpose." Romans 8:28 (NKJV)

"For I know the plans and thoughts that I have for you,' says the LORD, '**plans for peace and well-being** and not for disaster, to give you a future and a hope."
Jeremiah 29:11 (AMP)

"Trust in the Lord with all your heart and lean not on your own understanding; **in all your ways submit to him**, and he will make your paths straight. Do not be wise in your own eyes; fear the Lord and shun evil. **This will bring health to your body and nourishment to your bones**." Proverbs 3:5-8 (NIV)

And God can never go back on His Word, which means that we can trust Him – even when we don't receive immediate healing.

Does God Want You To Be Well?

If illness can be used for our good and for God's glory, and if physical healing in this lifetime is not a guarantee, does God want us to be well?

Jesus says that the devil comes to steal, kill and destroy; but Jesus came so that we may have **abundant life**:

> "The thief comes only to steal and kill and destroy. I came that they may have life and have it abundantly."
> John 10:10 (ESV)

God allowed His only Son to die so that we would be made well. Jesus was beaten, abused, whipped, ridiculed, mocked, shanked, humiliated, and ultimately murdered. Jesus took all of that punishment for us, and because of His sacrifice we are healed today.

> "But He was wounded for our transgressions, He was crushed for our wickedness [our sin, our injustice, our wrongdoing]; **The punishment [required] for our well-being fell on Him, And by His stripes (wounds) we are healed**." Isaiah 53:5 (AMP)

Why was a punishment required for our well-being? **A just God requires just consequences for sin.** Law, and just consequences for breaking the law, is what actually allows *everyone* to be free. Here is a simple example: Imagine that there are no laws against burglary, and that anybody could just walk into your house and take your stuff without legal consequences. We have laws against the 'freedom' for burglars to rob homes, so that the freedoms of the general population can be protected. Jesus says,

DID YOU KNOW?
God cannot go back on His Word. When Jesus gave His life, God's Word from the Old Testament was fulfilled.[1] (Num. 23:19; Heb. 9:12; Rom. 10:4)

> "**Do not think that I came to do away with or undo the Law [of Moses] or the [writings of the] Prophets; I did not come to destroy but to fulfill.** For I assure you and most solemnly say to you, until heaven and earth pass

away, not the smallest letter or stroke [of the pen] will pass from the Law until all things [which it foreshadows] are accomplished." Matthew 5:17-18 (AMP)

The phrase 'Law and Prophets' refers to the entire Old Testament (*See Chapter 14, Bible Facts & Abbreviation Guide*). The Old Testament includes many "rules and regulations" from the time before Jesus on topics like blood sacrifice, eating unclean foods, and tithing. These are known as the Law, or the Law of Moses. **Since Jesus fulfilled the Old Testament Law perfectly, law-keeping is no longer the path to righteousness. Jesus Christ is now our only path to righteousness.**[2] That is why we no longer have to sacrifice goats at the altar, or have diet restrictions, or give a set amount of money to the church. Jesus satisfied all of this when He died on the cross. Jesus was the only One capable of doing this, because He is God in the flesh and because He never sinned. That is why Jesus is the ultimate sacrifice.

"He went **once for all** into the Holy Place [the Holy of Holies of heaven, into the presence of God], and **not through the blood of goats and calves, but through His own blood, having obtained and secured eternal redemption** [that is, the salvation of all who personally believe in Him as Savior]." Hebrews 9:12 (AMP)

"**For Christ *is* the end of the law for righteousness** to everyone who believes." Romans 10:4 (NKJV)

"**Know that a person is not justified by the works of the law, but by faith in Jesus Christ.** So we, too, have put our faith in Christ Jesus that we may be justified by faith in Christ and not by the works of the law, **because by the works of the law no one will be justified**."
Galatians 2:16 (NIV)

Our God is so good and just that He not only accepts, **but provides and becomes,** an unblemished lamb offered up on our behalf. God has gracefully provided a means for our salvation and healing through Christ's sacrifice. The price has already been paid; will we accept what Christ has done for us?

Do You Want To Be Well?

Because Jesus paid the ultimate price for us on the cross and our bodies are now temples of the Holy Spirit, we have been given the righteous task of providing a healthy, well-maintained place for Him in which to reside:

> "Do you not know that your bodies are temples of the Holy Spirit, who is in you, whom you have received from God? **You are not your own; you were bought at a price. Therefore honor God with your bodies.**"
> 1 Corinthians 6:19-20 (NIV)

This includes maintaining our physical and mental well-being by honoring God with our lifestyle choices, behaviors, and even our thoughts. Negative words (including thoughts that we speak about ourselves) can cause sickness and prevent healing, whereas positive words (and thoughts) have the power to heal:

> "There is one who speaks rashly like the thrusts of a sword, But the tongue of the wise brings **healing**." Proverbs 12:18 (AMP)

> "A soothing tongue [speaking words that build up and encourage] is a **tree of life**, But a perversive tongue [speaking words that overwhelm and depress] crushes the spirit." Proverbs 15:4 (AMP)

> "A joyful heart is **good medicine**, but a crushed spirit dries up the bones." Proverbs 17:22 (ESV)

The effects of negative words and sounds on living things, versus the effects of positive words and sounds on living things, are visibly and tangibly measurable. Our thoughts and words, as well as the content we choose to intake, all have the power to impact us on a physical level.

In addition to harmful thoughts about ourselves, negative thinking also includes the darkness of our imaginations. It is so important to take our thoughts captive (*See Chapter 9, Self-Esteem*) and protect our eye gates and ear gates (*See Chapter 7, Fighting & Arguing*). If we don't, we are living a punishment inside of our minds while reacting with real-life stress and fear. Our thoughts might be imagined, but the effects of our thoughts on our physical bodies is very real.

What Are You Willing To Do To Be Well?

Are you willing to give up bad habits, negative thinking patterns, unforgiveness, resentment, anger, fear... and live by the Word of God? In the book of John, Jesus asks a paralyzed man if he wants to be healed:

> "When Jesus saw him lying there and knew that he had already been there a long time, he said to him, **'Do you want to be healed?'**" John 5:6 (ESV)

Why would Jesus ask that when the answer seems obvious? Of course the man wants to be healed, just as you and I want to be healed – but there is a deeper meaning behind that question. Jesus is not only asking (the man, or you, or I) if we want our current physical ailments to cease; He is asking if we desire a deeper-level spiritual healing. He is asking if we are willing to go outside of our comfort zone and have a closer relationship with Him. Our relationship with Jesus is directly related to our well-being.

We must ask ourselves this question, then, and be honest: **Do we really want to be healed?** Or are we afraid of deeper-level healing because we don't want to give up our bad habits, let go of unforgiveness and resentment, or lose the pleasure we may get from receiving sympathy or being taken care of when we're ill?

Sometimes it's hard to do anything when we feel sick or weak or ashamed, but the best thing we can do is to pray and to ask for prayer. The book of James gives this advice:

> "Is anyone among you suffering? Let him pray. Is anyone cheerful? Let him sing praise. Is anyone among you sick? Let him call for the elders of the church, and let them pray over him, anointing him with oil in the name of the Lord. **And the prayer of faith will save the one who is**

sick, and the Lord will raise him up. And if he has committed sins, he will be forgiven. **Therefore, confess your sins to one another and pray for one another, that you may be healed. The prayer of a righteous person has great power as it is working."** James 5:13-16 (ESV)

Understanding the importance of prayer, and actually remembering to pray, can be difficult as a new Christian. Prayer might be a completely different way of handling situations than what you have been used to. As an atheist, I didn't understand or believe in prayer at all. Now I know why:

"And I will ask the Father, and He will give you another Helper (Comforter, Advocate, Intercessor—Counselor, Strengthener, Standby), to be with you forever— **the Spirit of Truth, whom the world cannot receive [and take to its heart] because it does not see Him or know Him, *but* you know Him because He (the Holy Spirit) remains with you *continually* and will be in you.**"
John 14:16-17 (AMP)

As born-again believers in Christ, we have the awesome Spirit of God living within us. We now have the ability to understand God's Word as Truth.

DID YOU KNOW?

The Power of the Holy Spirit

The same Spirit that allows us to recognize God's Word as Truth – the Holy Spirit – is the same Spirit that raised Jesus from the grave, and the same Spirit that lives within us and gives life to our flesh.
(John 14:17; Romans 8:11)

"But if Christ is in you, then even though your body is subject to death because of sin, the Spirit gives life because of righteousness. And if the Spirit of him who raised Jesus from the dead is living in you, **he who raised Christ from the dead will also give life to your mortal bodies because of his Spirit who lives in you.**" Romans 8:10-11 (NIV)

And while we may be able to recognize God's Word as Truth, our past experiences can make it difficult for us to have faith and not to doubt God's plan and process. Where do you stand when it comes to faith vs. doubt?

Have Faith And Do Not Doubt

Do you have faith, but also doubt? If so, then you are in good company. Many of us have struggled with faithlessness and doubt, even Jesus' own disciples:

> "When they came to the crowd, a man approached Jesus and knelt before him. 'Lord, have mercy on my son,' he said. 'He has seizures and is suffering greatly. He often falls into the fire or into the water. **I brought him to your disciples, but they could not heal him.**' 'You unbelieving and perverse generation,' Jesus replied, 'how long shall I stay with you? How long shall I put up with you? Bring the boy here to me.' **Jesus rebuked the demon, and it came out of the boy, and he was healed at that moment.** Then the disciples came to Jesus in private and asked, 'Why couldn't we drive it out?' He replied, **'Because you have so little faith. Truly I tell you, if you have faith as small as a mustard seed, you can say to this mountain, 'Move from here to there,' and it will move. Nothing will be impossible for you.'**" Matthew 17:14-20 (NIV)

> "Early in the morning, as Jesus was on his way back to the city, he was hungry. Seeing a fig tree by the road, he went up to it but found nothing on it except leaves. Then he said to it, 'May you never bear fruit again!' Immediately the tree withered. When the disciples saw this, they were amazed. 'How did the fig tree wither so quickly?' they asked. Jesus replied, **'Truly I tell you, if you have faith and do not doubt, not only can you do what was done to the fig tree, but also you can say to this mountain, 'Go, throw yourself into the sea,' and it will be done. If you believe, you will receive whatever you ask for in prayer.'**" Matthew 21:18-22 (NIV)

Jesus says 'have faith' *and* 'do not doubt'. Throughout the New Testament, **faith is a prerequisite to healing** (and not necessarily the faith of the person being healed!) Only a little faith is required to move mountains – but we must **believe** that the mountains will move.

> "But he must ask [for wisdom] in faith, **without doubting** [God's willingness to help], for the one who doubts is like a billowing surge of the sea that is blown about and tossed by the wind." James 1:6 (AMP)

Jesus Himself says that we can ask, believe and receive all of the things we pray for. **As Christians and students of the Word, we know that this means praying, believing, and receiving in accordance with God's will.** The more we mature in Christ and study God's Word, the easier it is to discern God's will.

> "Therefore, I say to you, all things for which you pray and ask, believe that you have received them, and they will be granted to you. And whenever you stand praying, forgive, if you have anything against anyone, so that your Father who is in heaven will also forgive you for your offenses. [But if you do not forgive, neither will your Father who is in heaven forgive your offenses.]"
> Mark 11:24-26 (NASB)

Jesus also tells us that when we pray, we are to forgive. Unresolved issues and unforgiveness are huge blockers of our ability to receive healing.

<u>Act On Your Faith</u>

If faith is a prerequisite to healing, then how do we act on our faith? There are many beautiful examples of healing as a result of a person's faith sprinkled throughout the New Testament. Some of them include (and there are many more!) the story of the faith of one leper (Luke 17:11-19); the story of Aeneas who got up, rolled up his mat, and was healed (Acts 9:32-35); the story of two blind men who went against the crowd and were healed (Matthew 30:29-34); the story of the woman who touched the hem of Jesus' garment (Mark 5:25-34). But my personal favorite is the story of the Centurion's faith:

> "As Jesus went into Capernaum, a centurion came up to Him, begging Him [for help], and saying, 'Lord, my servant is lying at home paralyzed, with intense and terrible, tormenting pain.' Jesus said to him, 'I will come and heal him.' But the centurion replied to Him, **'Lord, I am not worthy to have You come under my roof, but only say the word, and my servant will be healed.** For I also am a man subject to authority [of a higher rank], with soldiers subject to me; and I say to one, 'Go!' and he goes, and to another, 'Come!' and he comes, and to my slave, 'Do this!' and he does it.' When Jesus heard this, He was amazed and said to those who were following Him, **'I tell you truthfully, I have not found such great faith [as this] with anyone in Israel... Then Jesus said to the centurion, 'Go; it will be done for you as you have believed.' And the servant was restored to health at that very hour**."Matthew 8:5-10,13 (AMP)

The centurion's faith was enough to heal another person (who wasn't even physically present)! We don't know whether the servant had faith or believed that he would be healed beforehand; we only know that the Centurion believed that the servant could be healed by Jesus' authority. **Believing is an act of faith.**

We have been instructed to have faith and not to doubt, and we have been given the authority to stand against the enemy in Jesus' name (including when it comes to our healing):

> "I assure you and most solemnly say to you, **anyone who believes in Me [as Savior] will also do the things that I do; and he will do even greater things than these** [in extent and outreach], because I am going to the Father. And I will do whatever you ask in My name [as My representative], this I will do, so that the Father may be glorified and celebrated in the Son. **If you ask Me anything in My name [as My representative], I will do it.**" John 14:12-14 (AMP)

"Whoever believes and is baptized will be saved, but whoever does not believe will be condemned. **And these signs will accompany those who believe:** in my name they will cast out demons; they will speak in new tongues; they will pick up serpents with their hands; and if they drink any deadly poison, it will not hurt them; **they will lay their hands on the sick, and they will recover.'**" Mark 16:16-18 (ESV)

Gifts Of The Spirit

Do these 'signs' (also known as gifts of the Spirit) still exist today, or did they pass away with the old times? The Bible tells us that **the same God works all things in all people**, meaning all those who are indwelled with the Holy Spirit. It doesn't say 'just the Apostles', or 'just the people of Jesus' time'! We are each given different gifts of the Spirit, assigned to us by God as He sees fit, for His glory and for the good of His people.

DID YOU KNOW?
Through Christ Jesus, we have the authority to stand against the enemy's attacks on our physical bodies today. (Mark 16:16-18)

"**There are different kinds of gifts, but the same Spirit distributes them. There are different kinds of service, but the same Lord. There are different kinds of working, but in all of them and in everyone it is the same God at work.** Now to each one the manifestation of the Spirit is given for the common good. To one there is given through the Spirit a message of wisdom, to another a message of knowledge by means of the same Spirit, to another faith by the same Spirit, **to another gifts of healing** by that one Spirit, to another miraculous powers, to another prophecy, to another distinguishing between spirits, to another speaking in different kinds of tongues, and to still another the interpretation of tongues. **All these are the work of one and the same Spirit, and he distributes them to each one, just as he determines.**"
1 Corinthians 12:4-11 (NIV)

DID YOU KNOW?
NEVER COME IN YOUR OWN NAME! The Holy Spirit of God living within you is the part of you that comes against the enemy. The part of you that is YOU cannot stand against the enemy. We are representatives of Christ, because Christ is living within us; therefore we can only come against the devil in the Name of Jesus. (John 15:5)

Apart from Christ, we can do nothing. **We do not** have the authority to control God or to control grace. We do have the authority to put on the Spiritual Armor of God (Ephesians 6:10-18) and boldly rebuke the devil in the name of Jesus. We do have the authority to align ourselves with Christ, and not with the symptoms of ailment. We do have the authority to stop making pain and sickness an idol.

"I am the vine; you are the branches. If you remain in me and I in you, you will bear much fruit; **apart from me you can do nothing**." John 15:5 (NIV)

The Lord gives and the Lord takes away as He sees fit (Job 1:21), so any gift that we are given belongs to God and therefore can be taken away at His discretion at any time. We deserve nothing, and we can earn nothing – not even the breath in our lungs. It's the simple humility that God is the glue that holds ALL of this together, and that the breath in our lungs and the beating of our hearts only continues because God wills it to. This type of thinking leads to a constant, immense gratitude for salvation.

<u>The Lord's Benefits</u>

The psalmist (David, in this case) reminds us of the Lord's benefits:

"Bless the Lord, my soul,
And all that is within me, bless His holy name.
Bless the Lord, my soul,
And do not forget any of His benefits;
Who pardons all your guilt,
Who heals all your diseases;
Who redeems your life from the pit,
Who crowns you with favor and compassion;
Who satisfies your years with good things,

So that your youth is renewed like the eagle."
Psalm 103:2-5 (NASB)

God's Word itself has the power to heal:

"He sent out **his word** and **healed them**, and delivered them from their destruction." Psalm 107:20 (ESV)

"My son, **be attentive to my words**; incline your ear to my sayings. Let them not escape from your sight; keep them within your heart. **For they are life to those who find them, and healing to all their flesh**."
Proverbs 4:20-22 (ESV)

We will be healed, in God's own way and in God's own timing, for our good and for His glory.

<u>The Glue</u>

Sometimes following the Word of God is easier said than done. I don't always have all the answers, and I'm not always holding it all together. When we find ourselves starting to unravel, we must remember that **Jesus is the glue that holds all things together**. We don't have to hold it together. We just have to have **faith** and **believe** that Jesus is holding it together; that He is good, righteous and just; and that His way is always the best way. We can pass the baton over to Him and rest easy knowing that He is doing a much better job than any of us ever could.

"For in him all things were created: things in heaven and on earth, visible and invisible, whether thrones or powers or rulers or authorities; **all things have been created through him and for him.** He is before all things, **and in him all things hold together**." Colossians 1:16-17 (NIV)

CHAPTER 12

DO YOU HAVE TO GO TO CHURCH?

The idea of going to church can be overwhelming, especially if you happen to be an introvert with little-to-no church experience (hello!) – But do we have to go to church to live the Christian life, or to get to heaven?

Is Going To Church A Biblical Requirement?

What if you work on Sundays? What if you have health issues? What if you've already tried going to church and you had a bad experience?

The truth is that there is nothing we can do to earn a place in the Kingdom of Heaven; therefore, going to church is not a Biblical requirement for salvation:

> "For it is by **grace** [God's remarkable compassion and favor drawing you to Christ] that you have been **saved** [actually delivered from judgment and given eternal life] through **faith**. And this [salvation] is not of yourselves [not through your own effort], **but it is the [undeserved, gracious] gift of God; not as a result of [your] works [nor your attempts to keep the Law], so that no one will [be able to] boast or take credit in any way [for his salvation]."** Ephesians 2:8-9 (AMP)

The only requirement for salvation is faith in Jesus Christ. Having a personal relationship with Christ is more important than the religious rules set forth by men. For example, church attendance shouldn't occur at the expense of our health or safety; nor should we remain in a community that does not have Christ at its head, or that misrepresents the heart and character of God. Finally, going to church should not be an end in itself. It's far better to have a relationship with Christ and not go to church, than to go to church and not have a relationship with Christ.

If having a relationship with Christ is personal, then why go to church at all?

Do Not Neglect To Meet Together

While the only way to salvation is through Jesus, and not the church, the Bible teaches us to meet together as believers for encouragement, worship, instruction, prayer and fellowship. Meeting together is a natural way for us to learn, to support one another, and to grow in our faith:

> "Let us seize and hold tightly the confession of our hope without wavering, for He who promised is reliable and trustworthy and faithful [to His word]; **and let us consider [thoughtfully] how we may encourage one another to love and to do good deeds, not forsaking our meeting together [as believers for worship and instruction],** as is the habit of some, but encouraging one another; and all the more [faithfully] as you see the day [of Christ's return] approaching."
> Hebrews 10:23-25 (AMP)

> "They devoted themselves to the apostles' teaching **and to fellowship, to the breaking of bread and to prayer."**
> Acts 2:42 (NIV)

> "As iron sharpens iron, so one person sharpens another."
> Proverbs 27:17 (NIV)

The importance of people and community is significant in the Bible. Check out Jesus' answer when He was asked which one of the Bible's commandments is the greatest:

> "Jesus replied: 'Love the Lord your God with all your heart and with all your soul and with all your mind.' This is the first and greatest commandment. And the second is

like it: 'Love your neighbor as yourself.' All the Law and the Prophets hang on these two commandments." Matthew 22:37-40 (NIV)

The entire Bible points to loving God and loving people. We shouldn't stay home from church out of fear (of people; of being judged; of having to participate). You never know how God is going to use you. Sometimes we need, and sometimes we're needed.

ACTIONABLE INSIGHT

The Lord is perfect; people are not. Do not let the imperfections of *people* deter you from the Lord, or prevent you from going to church.

Theoretically, we don't "have to" go to church. We could watch sermons online and read the Bible from the comfort of our own homes. But how disciplined are we, and what is the quality of our solitary worship and Bible study? What we should really be asking is: How much spiritual growth can I achieve on my own; and what are my deeper reasons for not wanting to go to church?

<u>The Grand Tapestry</u>

"So that we are no longer children [spiritually immature], tossed back and forth [like ships on a stormy sea] and carried about by every wind of [shifting] doctrine, by the cunning and trickery of [unscrupulous] men, by the deceitful scheming of people ready to do anything [for personal profit]. But speaking the truth in love [in all things—both our speech and our lives expressing His truth], let us grow up in all things into Him [following His example] who is the Head—Christ. **From Him the whole body [the church, in all its**

DID YOU KNOW?

We are now a part of the grand tapestry woven together by the Lord, and *our part* in it working properly leads to unity and maturity in the *entire body* of Christ.

various parts], joined and knitted firmly together by what every joint supplies, when each part is working properly, causes the body to grow and mature, building itself up in [unselfish] love." Ephesians 4:14-16 (AMP)

Whether we realize it or not, we have something to offer when we go to church. We may feel insignificant, but even our little role makes a huge impact in the body of Christ.

Unity And Diversity In The Body

There is a reason that God made you who you are, and why you've had the past that you've had. There is beauty and purpose in our differences. God made us exactly who we are for our own good, for the greater good, and for His own glory; and we are stationed in life at the exact time, surrounded by the exact people, that God wills. The Bible says that the church is one body with many members, just like our human body as a whole is made up of many different parts:

"For just as the body is one and yet has many parts, and all the parts, though many, form [only] one body, so it is with Christ. For by one [Holy] Spirit we were all baptized into one body, [spiritually transformed—united together] whether Jews or Greeks (Gentiles), slaves or free, and we were all made to drink of one [Holy] Spirit [since the same Holy Spirit fills each life]. For the [human] body does not consist of one part, but of many [limbs and organs]. If the foot says, 'Because I am not a hand, I am not a part of the body,' is it not on the contrary still a part of the body? If the ear says, 'Because I am not an eye, I am not a part of the body,' is it not on the contrary still a part of the body? If the whole body were an eye, where would the hearing be? If the whole [body] were an ear, where would the sense of smell be? But now [as things really are], **God has placed and arranged the parts in the body, each one of them, just as He willed and saw fit** [with the best balance of function]. If they all were a single organ, where would [the rest of] the body be? But now [as things really are] there are many parts [different limbs and organs], but a single body. The eye cannot say to the hand, 'I have no need of you,' nor again the head to the feet, 'I have no need of you.' But quite the contrary, the parts of the body that seem to be weaker are [absolutely] necessary; and as for those parts of the body which we consider less honorable, these we treat with greater honor; and our less presentable parts are treated with greater modesty, while our more presentable parts do not require it. But God has combined the [whole] body, giving greater honor to that part which lacks it, so that there would be no division or discord in the body [that is, lack of adaptation of the parts to each other], but that the parts may have the same concern for one another. **And if one member suffers, all the parts share the suffering; if one member is honored, all rejoice with it. Now you [collectively] are Christ's body, and individually [you are] members of it [each with his own special purpose and function]."** 1 Corinthians 12:12-27 (AMP)

<u>Gifts Of Grace</u>

There is beauty and power in having multiple Holy Spirit-filled people gathered together in one place. God manifests through His people, including you and me, and we have all been given different gifts of grace:

"For as in one body we have many members, and the members do not all have the same function, so we, though many, are one body in Christ, and individually members one of another. Having gifts that differ according to the grace given to us, let us use them: if prophecy, in proportion to our faith; if service, in our serving; the one who teaches, in his teaching; the one who exhorts, in his exhortation; the one who contributes, in generosity; the one who leads, with zeal; the one who does acts of mercy, with cheerfulness."
Romans 12:4-8 (ESV)

Finding The Right Church

Finding the perfect church is impossible. There is no perfect church, because churches are run by people, and people are imperfect. But you can find the RIGHT church for you, based on where you are right now (in your walk with Christ, as well as your physical location).

1. **Try a Variety of Churches**

There are many kinds of churches and worship styles. Try out a few places and see what works for you. Being a former atheist, I didn't know that there were different types of Christian churches or "denominations," so I had to try a variety of them in order to figure out what I liked and what I didn't like. What I found out is that there are churches that worship hard but read very little scripture, and churches that read a lot of scripture but worship very little. Some churches have more fellowship time than others. I like a happy medium: Genuine praise and worship; strong Biblical teaching; and time for fellowship.

2. **Try Churches Based on Location**

Check out places that are close to where you live. Search Maps and see what comes up near you. Most churches even post their mission statements online, so you can go to their webpage or social media and check them out ahead of time.

3. **Pray**

Not every church comes up online or on Maps. Pray and ask for God's direction and guidance in finding the right church.

Take Away From Every Service

No matter what church you go to, it's your job to take something away from the service. Going to church is not always enjoyable or easy. Sometimes it's boring and you'd rather be home watching football. But it's our job as students of the Word to listen for God's voice and to tune out the other stuff. Try not to focus on the person delivering the message, but focus on the message that God is delivering to you through that person.

ACTIONABLE INSIGHT

Find at least one thing to take away from every church service. Listen for God's voice and pay attention to what moves you. Take notes and write down scripture references to look up in your Bible at home.

Not All Churches Are On Maps

I prayed and tried every church on Maps, and still couldn't find one I liked. I was starting to feel defeated. Why weren't my prayers being answered? Didn't God want me in church? I sat down at the bus stop and vented about it to a stranger.

"You should come to my church," she said, "it's right down the street," and she gave me the address.

Sunday came. I put the address into my GPS and rode the bus just past where I had vented to the girl before. When the bus arrived at the correct stop, a man and I both got off. The bus drove away and I looked around: No church. It was just me and the man standing there in the middle of the street. There were a few office buildings and low-budget food places around, but it was pretty desolate. The man started walking and, not knowing what else to do, I started walking. He began to cross the street when suddenly a car full of people came screeching to a stop in front of him. They rolled down the window and hollered, "Where da church at?" The man pointed to one of the buildings hidden on the other side of the street, and then proceeded to walk towards it. I followed him inside.

I had my own, personal escort right into the front doors of the church. I would have never found that place if I hadn't first vented to the girl at the bus stop, and then been lead inside by the man. I began going to that church weekly. Eventually I met my husband, and we got married there. Time passed and we started a family, moved away, and began the church search all over again. By the grace of God, we found a great church near our home, and most of the people that go there are our neighbors. Is it perfect? No; but it is perfect for me and my family, where we are right now.

CHAPTER 13

HOW TO READ THE BIBLE

You may have encountered some challenges with reading the Bible, especially if you didn't grow up in church. In my case, the scriptures and stories were unfamiliar, I didn't understand the old-timey language, and I couldn't keep track of who and what I was reading about.

Fortunately, there are three important steps you can take to make reading the Bible easier and more enjoyable:

1. Ask, Seek, Knock

The first few times I tried reading the Bible, it was horribly boring, confusing, and frustrating for me. It had language, abbreviations, and italicized words like I had not seen in any other book. As a result, I felt dumb and I didn't want to read it.

If this sounds familiar, **relax**. God wants us to desire His Word. The Bible is called God's *Living* Word because God is supernatural, and His Word is supernatural – which means that **God has the ability to reveal His Word to us supernaturally.**

> "Ask and it will be given to you; seek and you will find; knock and the door will be opened to you. For everyone who asks receives; the one who seeks finds; and to the one who knocks, the door will be opened."
> Matthew 7:7-8 (NIV)

2. Pray

Ask God for understanding, direction, and a readied heart to receive His Word. When praying, thank God and refer to the scriptures often (*See Chapter 2, How To Pray*):

Lord, thank You for Your Living Word. Please guide me and give me wisdom and understanding as I study Your Word. Ready me to receive Your Word, that I may be good soil; and plant the seed of Your Word in my heart, that it may produce good fruit. Point me in the right direction, remove the scales from my eyes, and reveal to me what You would have me to know. Thank You for the opportunity to get to know You through Your Living Word, and thank You for Your hand and guidance over my life. In the name of Jesus, Amen.

DID YOU KNOW?

The Holy Spirit

Once we receive Christ into our hearts, we are filled with the Holy Spirit. The Holy Spirit is our guide and helps us in understanding the Bible and remembering the scriptures. The Holy Spirit can recall scriptures that we didn't even realize we knew! (John 14:26)

3. Get the Right Bible

I stopped reading my Bible for a while because all I had was a stinky old King James Version. I hated reading it. I couldn't understand the Old English and it smelled like a 1970's garage sale. Finally, I went online and looked around for exactly what I wanted.

I ended up getting two Bibles. (These are the ones I actually own and use; I have no other affiliation.)

The NIV, KJV, NASB, AMP Parallel Bible (Zondervan): This Bible has four reliable translations side-by-side so you can compare the different wordings for a fuller understanding of the scriptures.

The Action Bible (David C Cook): Sure, it's a comic book Bible recommended for kids ages 8 to 12 – but it's beautifully illustrated and arranged chronologically, which is incredibly helpful for a better understanding of the big picture.

I look at the pictures in the Action Bible while reading the Parallel Bible at the same time. Whatever works for you – do it! **There is no wrong way to study the Bible.**

ACTIONABLE INSIGHT

Get a Bible (or two) that you actually ENJOY reading.

Which Translation Is Best?

There are different approaches to translating the Bible. Here are some common ones:

Word-For-Word – Also known as Formal Equivalence, Word-For-Word translations aim to preserve as much from the original Bible text as possible, resulting in a more literal translation.[1]

Thought-For-Thought – Also known as Functional Equivalence or Dynamic Equivalence, this approach aims to maintain the meaning of the original Bible text, while re-wording it for understandability.[2]

Paraphrase – This type of translation is a complete retelling of the original Bible text.[3]

My Top 5 Picks for Reliable Bible Translations:

ESV – English Standard Version (Word-For-Word)
AMP – Amplified Version (Word-For-Word)
NIV – New International Version (Thought-For-Thought)
NASB – New American Standard Bible (Word-For-Word)
NKJV/KJV – New King James Version/King James Version (Word-For-Word)

There are lots of Bibles to choose from, so stick with a standard, reliable version that is easy for you to read. If you still can't decide which translation to choose, try a parallel Bible.

What About Bible Apps?

It's ok to use Bible apps as a study tool, but the good ol' printed Bible in a standard translation is most reliable. Printed Bibles are edited with the highest scrutiny, and they cannot be easily modified. Plus, it gives your eyes a break from the screen for a little while.

Book, Chapter, Verse

Scripture notations can be confusing when you are new to the Bible.

What do the names and numbers mean?

- Every book of the Bible has a Name, a Chapter, and Verses
- Some books of the Bible also have a Number
- Books are only numbered when they are part of a series
- Bible book Names are often abbreviated
- Each Bible Verse is numbered
- A Verse is not necessarily a single sentence

What do the dots and dashes mean?

How it's written: **John 1:1-4**
What it means: **The Book of John, Chapter One, Verses One through Four**

How it's written: **1 John 1:4**
What it means: **The Book of First John, Chapter One, Verse Four**

How it's written: **Romans 10:9-10,13**
What it means: **The Book of Romans, Chapter Ten, Verses Nine through Ten, and Verse Thirteen**

How it's written: **Matthew 13**
What it means: **The Book of Matthew, Chapter Thirteen, The Entire Chapter**

Random Italics?

Why *do* certain Bible passages *have* randomly italicized *words*?

The italicized words in some translations of the Bible were not in the original Bible text.[4] These words were added by translators in order to make the text more understandable in English, and then italicized to differentiate them from the original text.[5] Here is an example:

> "Then God said, 'Let the earth bring forth grass, the herb *that* yields seed, *and* the fruit tree *that* yields fruit according to its kind, whose seed *is* in itself, on the earth'; and it was so." Genesis 1:11 (NKJV)

Since the words are italicized to indicate that they have been added to the text and not for emphasis, no inflection is required when you're reading them; however, if you want to use inflection, go right ahead!

CHAPTER 14

BIBLE FACTS & ABBREVIATION GUIDE

The books of the Bible were written by **40 men** over a period of **1500 years.**[1]

The Bible consists of **66 total books** (1,189 chapters; 31,102 verses):
-The Old Testament has **39 books** (929 chapters; 23,145 verses)
-The New Testament has **27 books** (260 chapters; 7,957 verses)[2]

The books of the Bible are divided into **Old Testament** (before the birth of Jesus) and **New Testament** (the life, death and resurrection of Jesus).

The Old Testament can be broken down into parts: The Law of Moses, the Prophets, and the Psalms.[3]

The Psalms are often a sub-category of the Prophets. Because Jews often viewed any writer of Scripture as a prophet, the entire Jewish Bible (the Old Testament) is typically referred to as the Law and Prophets.[4]

The Pentateuch are the first five books of the Bible: Genesis, Exodus, Leviticus, Numbers, and Deuteronomy. Jews refer to these books as the Torah (meaning "instruction" or "teaching" in Hebrew).[5] Written primarily by Moses, they are known as the books of the Law. The rest of the books in the Old Testament are known as the Prophets.[7]

DID YOU KNOW?
Pentateuch (ˈpen-te-ˌtük) means "five books" in Greek.[6]

Same Name

Some books in the Bible have the same name, and are written by the same man. Some books in the Bible have the same name, but are written by different men. Some men in the Bible have the same name. Some men in the Bible were renamed. Confusing, much?

Real-life comparison: My husband and my brother have the same first name, which can be confusing until you get to know them. In the same way, becoming familiar with the people and stories in the Bible will help you to make sense of the duplicate names.

Examples:

The book of ***John*** is not the same as the book of ***1 John***. **John the Baptist** wrote the book of John. **John the Apostle** wrote the books of 1 John, 2 John and 3 John. They are two different guys. Here is what they probably looked like:

John the Baptist / © Jade Creighton

John the Apostle / © Jade Creighton

John the Baptist ≠ John the Apostle

In the **New Testament**, there is a guy named **Saul of Tarsus**. He is renamed **Paul** (Acts 13:9). He becomes one of Jesus' Disciples and goes on to write the majority of the New Testament. Over a thousand years before that, there was a completely different guy in the **Old Testament** named **King Saul** (1 Samuel 9). He is crabby and he doesn't like it when people think he's Paul (AKA, Saul of Tarsus) from the New Testament.

Paul the Disciple / © Jade Creighton

King Saul / © Jade Creighton

Saul (New Testament) = Paul
King Saul (Old Testament) ≠ Paul

Peter, another one of Jesus' disciples from the New Testament, was also renamed. **Peter** is his new name. His old name was **Simon** (Matt. 10:2; Mark 3:16; Luke 6:14). He doesn't get a drawing.

Simon = Peter

In the Old Testament, there was a guy named **Jacob**. Jacob wrestled with God (Genesis 32:22-32) and was renamed **Israel**. In the Bible, Israel sometimes refers to a physical location, but sometimes Israel refers to the guy who used to be named Jacob.

Jacob (person) = Israel (same person, new name)
Israel (location) = descendents of Jacob

Common Bible Book Abbreviations

Note: Most Bible book abbreviations are only three or four letters long, so shorter book names are often unabbreviated.

Acts: Ac, Act
Amos: Am, Amo
1 Chronicles: I Ch, I Chr
2 Chronicles: II Ch, II Chr
Colossians: Col
1 Corinthians: I Co, I Cor
2 Corinthians: II Co, II Cor
Daniel: Da, Dan
Deuteronomy: Deu, Deut
Ecclesiastes: Ec, Ecc, Eccl
Ephesians: Ep, Eph
Esther: Est, Esth
Exodus: Ex, Exo, Exod
Ezekiel: Ez, Eze, Ezk
Ezra: Ezr
Galatians: Ga, Gal
Genesis: Ge, Gen
Habakkuk: Hab
Haggai: Hag
Hebrews: He, Heb
Hosea: Ho, Hos
Isaiah: Is, Isa
James: Jam
Jeremiah: Jer, Jere
Job: Jo
Joel: Joe
John: Jn
1 John: I Jo, I Joh
2 John: II Jo, II Joh
3 John: III Jo, III Joh
Jonah: Jon, Jona
Joshua: Jos, Josh
Jude: Jud
Judges: Judg
1 Kings: I Ki, I Kin
2 Kings: II Ki, II Kin
Lamentations: La, Lam
Leviticus: Lev
Luke: Lu, Luk
Malachi: Mal
Mark: Mar
Matthew: Mat, Matt
Micah: Mi, Mic, Mica
Nahum: Na, Nah
Nehemiah: Ne, Neh
Numbers: Nu, Num
Obadiah: Ob, Oba
1 Peter: I Pe, I Pet
2 Peter: II Pe, II Pet
Philemon: Phm, Phile
Philippians: Phil, Phili
Proverbs: Pr, Pro, Prov
Psalms: Ps, Psa
Revelation: Re, Rev
Romans: Ro, Rom, Roma
Ruth: Ru, Rt
1 Samuel: I Sa, I Sam
2 Samuel: II Sa, II Sam
Song of Songs: SS, Song
1 Thessalonians: I Th, I The
2 Thessalonians: II Th, II The
1 Timothy: I Ti, I Tim
2 Timothy: II Ti, II Tim
Titus: Ti, Tit
Zechariah: Zch, Zech
Zephaniah: Zep, Zph, Zep

CHAPTER 15

ROAD TRIP TO REDEMPTION: TESTIMONY & CONCLUSION

I was raised atheist in East Detroit in the 90s. Growing up, my siblings and I were taught that people who believed in God were dumb, and that science and intellect were king. In middle school, I chose to do a research paper on Charles Darwin and the Theory of Evolution. Because I believed that all creation came from primordial sludge, I honestly thought that my life was no different than that of an insect. Once it was over, it was over forever. I didn't believe in Heaven and I didn't believe in Hell. I placed no value on my own life, because I truly believed that life had no purpose. I shut down any contradictory evidence. I believed what I was taught to believe, and in our house believing in a higher power was for the weak and simpleminded. We were taught that God was a fictitious character made up by people as a replacement for drug and alcohol addictions.

Everything you've heard about Detroit is probably true. It's a crime-ridden, burnt-down death hole. It's full of rich history, architecture, music, culture, and tough, creative people. It's a city of brawlers, and my family was a street brawling family. There is a haunting beauty to the place; I've left it, but it has never left me.

Detroit is full of people from all over the world. In my mid-twenties, I became roommates with a group of people from Nepal. They were a peaceful and religious people – the complete opposite of my family – and I admired them for it.

For weeks, we traveled together on a cross-country road trip, staying with Nepali friends and relatives all over America. Religion was a common part of daily life in the homes we visited, and it was discussed with ease and confidence. No one got offended, no one argued or debated. I witnessed religious activities such as praying, lighting incense, and regular fasting. It was fascinating; not one person we visited was an atheist. Seeing religion from a different perspective was what it took. **Suddenly I knew that God was real.**

I started to feel anxious and excited. There was no turning back now; I knew that I was a part of something bigger than me. I had heard about different religions, but I didn't know which one of them was right. **Most of what I had heard about Christianity was bad,** so I tried out the Hindu and Buddhist temples, the Jewish synagogue, and the Unitarian church.

I was skeptical of Hinduism because of the number of gods; the requirements for converting to Judaism scared the crap out of me; and the Unitarian church bored me so much that I actually fell asleep during service, repeatedly. But the Buddhist temple was nice…

I read a brief online history of the Buddha, and I read a book about a guy who had read the Tao Te Ching. That was good enough for me. **I had chosen my own path to enlightenment.**

My life, however, remained basically the same. The road trip ended in Northern California, and my Nepali friends went back to their respective homes in various states across the U.S. I stayed behind and got a job in the suburbs of San Francisco, achieving "balance" by working equally as hard as I partied. After a while, I did the typical modern relationship thing: Met a guy; dated; moved in. We lived together for nearly five years, and were in no hurry to get married.

Then one day everything changed. All of a sudden, I stopped approving of premarital sex. What happened to me?

As I sat alone thinking about it, I noticed an old Bible on the bookshelf. I had tried reading it before, but it was painfully boring and confusing to me. At that moment, I felt compelled to try reading it again – **but this time, I did something different.** I prayed first. It went something like this: "God, if you are real, and the Bible is the right path to You, allow me to understand what is written in it." **As I opened the book and began to read, I discovered something astonishing**: Everything that I read made perfect sense. I couldn't believe that I didn't understand it before! I spent the entire afternoon totally captivated. The Bible was the most fascinating book I had ever read.

I played it cool and didn't tell my boyfriend what was going on with me right away. For weeks I gave him excuses to avoid any serious physical contact, but finally he caught on. I hoped that after nearly five years of being together he would profess his undying love and propose, but he didn't. He left me.

My entire world for the past half a decade was gone. Now what? I was almost thirty by then, and I only had a couple of friends in California. I didn't want to be there anymore. That's when my sister asked me to move to Florida. She lived there with her husband and kids, and they offered me a place to stay. I had a choice: I could go back to Detroit, or I could start my life over again in yet another new state. I had nothing to lose and I missed my sister, so I decided to leave California and move to Florida.

Florida was completely different than what I was used to. It was scorching hot; the humidity made it hard not to sweat, which made it nearly impossible to wear makeup or to have good hair; and deodorant was basically useless. I was constantly getting sunburns and bug bites, and I developed pollen allergies. It felt like some sort of cruel and unusual punishment.

I discovered a little church within walking distance from my sister's house, and I began going there for Sunday service and Wednesday night Bible study. The congregation was small. One Sunday we all met up for lunch, and everyone was chit-chatting and telling stories when someone asked me when I was baptized. I answered nonchalantly that I wasn't baptized.

Everyone stopped what they were doing and looked at me. **They asked me if I was ready to commit my life to Jesus Christ.** As soon as I said yes it was like someone pulled the fire alarm. People quickly began wrapping up lunches and pushing in chairs. Someone yelled, "We're having an emergency baptism!" and then, "I have extra towels in my trunk!" Carpools were coordinated and people were offering to take pictures.

They drove me to a little beach off the local causeway. The pastor of the church was there, but surprisingly he didn't perform my baptism.

One of the young men from the congregation was nominated for the task. He asked me a few questions, told me to hold my nose, and dunked me into the salty beach water.

What happened next was totally unexpected. When I came up from the water, I felt like a completely new person. I was consumed with an overwhelming joy that was like fire in my soul. I thought that being baptized was just a pleasant formality in the Christian world, but it was as if my former "bad" self had been washed away. I was beaming as I made my way back to the beach. My church friends were all waiting there, clapping and cheering. Everyone shook my hand and gave me hugs. Then, after congratulating me and welcoming me to the faith, they drove me home.

The weeks ticked by and I continued to feel amazing. I expected everyone to keep checking in on how my post-baptism, life-on-fire was going, but they didn't. Normal life continued for everyone else, but my overwhelming joy could not be shaken. At first it was great, but after a while people started getting annoyed with me. Pretty soon I was under full enemy attack. Even total strangers would pass by and yell at me – but I didn't care, I had that unshakeable joy.

Eventually my mood evened out, but Jesus remained in my soul like an anchor. I figured it would wear off over time, but it only continued to grow stronger. I was no longer alone: I was a warrior fighting battles with a roaring lion by my side. My life had value and purpose, because I was made by a Creator by design with intention. I couldn't un-see it; evidence of God's existence was everywhere. But I wasn't just a believer in God now; I finally understood the meaning of *walking* with Christ and having a *relationship* with Jesus.

I used to roll my eyes when I heard people say things like that, and now I am one of them.

As an atheist, an infinite hole of sadness existed within me for many years of my life, and I thought it was normal. I tried to fill it with a number of worldly things. In knowing Jesus, the infinite hole of sadness has finally been filled.

I have been made alive in Christ.

Conclusion

Jesus came to call sinners, including ex-atheists, to repentance (Luke 5:32, Mark 2:17). People might think we've gone crazy and will even hate us for being Christians (Matthew 10:22; Mark 13:13, Luke 21:17), but nothing can ever separate us from the love of God in Christ (Romans 8:38-39). We can still be ourselves and be good Christians, because God uses our natural gifts and talents for His glory (1 Corinthians 12:4-11; Romans 12:6-8; 1 Peter 4:10-11). We are new creations in Christ, our pasts are forgotten, and our former selves are gone (2 Corinthians 5:17). We have been cleansed of our unrighteousness (1 John 1:9), and we are no longer condemned (Romans 8:1). God has given us His written Word (the Bible) and a Helper (the Holy Spirit, John 14:16-17) to guide us, and we are now part of an eternal brotherhood through Christ Jesus (John 1:12-13).

I hope and pray that this guide has helped you to understand some of the basics of Christianity, and to figure out some of the answers to life's tough questions. And remember:

DID YOU KNOW?
C.S. Lewis, revered Christian writer, was a former atheist.[1]

You Do Not Have To Be Perfect!

-Read the Bible;
-Trust the Word of God to be the truth;
-Understand that you are indwelled with the Holy Spirit; and
-Remember to pray.

"Here is a trustworthy saying that deserves full acceptance: Christ Jesus came into the world to save sinners—of whom I am the worst. But for that very reason I was shown mercy so that in me, the worst of sinners, Christ Jesus might display his immense patience as an example for those who would believe in him and receive eternal life. Now to the King eternal, immortal, invisible, the only God, be honor and glory for ever and ever. Amen." 1 Timothy 15-17 (NIV)

INDEX

NOTES

CHAPTER 2: HOW TO PRAY

1. Steven J. Cole, "Entering God's Holy Presence (Exodus 40:1-38)," bible.org, July 17, 2018, https://bible.org/seriespage/20-entering-god-s-holy-presence-exodus-401-38.

CHAPTER 3: DECISION MAKING

1. John M. Frame, "The Omnipotence, Omniscience, and Omnipresence of God," *The Gospel Coalition*, February 10, 2021, https://www.thegospelcoalition.org/essay/omnipotence-omniscience-omnipresence-god.

CHAPTER 4: HAMSTER-ON-WHEEL SYNDROME

1. Brannon Deibert, "What is Yoke in the Bible? Meaning of Jesus' Teaching," *Christianity.com*, April 6, 2022, https://www.christianity.com/jesus/life-of-jesus/teaching-and-messages/the-yoke-of-jesus-biblical-meaning-and-importance.html.
2. Deibert, "What is Yoke in the Bible? Meaning of Jesus' Teaching."
3. Deibert.

CHAPTER 5: TITHING WHEN YOU'RE BROKE

1. "What Does Tithe Mean? Bible Definition and References," *biblestudytools.com,* (n.d.), https://www.biblestudytools.com/dictionary/tithe.
2. "What Does Tithe Mean? Bible Definition and References."

CHAPTER 7: FIGHTING & ARGUING

1. "Is Satan / The Devil Omnipresent," *GotQuestions.org,* January 4, 2022, https://www.gotquestions.org/Satan-omnipresent.html.
2. Priscilla Shirer, *The Armor of God* (Nashville: Lifeway, 2022)

CHAPTER 9: SELF-ESTEEM

1. Priscilla Shirer, *The Armor of God* (Nashville: Lifeway, 2022), 178-179.

CHAPTER 10: FEAR OF GOD

1. "What Does it Mean to Have the Fear of God," *GotQuestions.org,* June 7, 2023, https://www.gotquestions.org/fear-God.html.
2. "What Does it Mean to Have the Fear of God."

CHAPTER 11: HEALING

1. John Piper, "How Christ Fulfilled and Ended the Old Testament Regime," *DesiringGod.org,* September 26, 2023, https://www.desiringgod.org/articles/how-christ-fulfilled-and-ended-the-old-testament-regime.

2. Piper, "How Christ Fulfilled and Ended the Old Testament Regime."

CHAPTER 13: HOW TO READ THE BIBLE

1. Tiffany Nicole, "Bible Translation Comparison: Top 10 most accurate Bible Translations," *Lavender Vines - a Christian Blog for Women*, 2021, https://lavendervines.com/bible-translation-comparison.

2. "What is Functional Equivalence in Bible Translation," *GotQuestions.org,* June 22, 2022, https://www.gotquestions.org/functional-equivalence.html.

3. Nicole, "Bible Translation Comparison: Top 10 most accurate Bible Translations."

4. "Why Do Many Bibles Show Some Words in Italics," *biblestudytools.org,* (n.d.), https://www.bibletools.org/index.cfm/fuseaction/Library.sr/CT/BQA/k/180/Why-Do-Many-Bibles-Show-Some-Words-Italics.htm.

5. "Chapters, Verses, Punctuation, Spelling, and Italics," *Religious Studies Center,* (n.d.), https://rsc.byu.edu/king-james-bible-restoration/chapters-verses-punctuation-spelling-italics.

CHAPTER 14: BIBLE FACTS & ABBREVIATION GUIDE

1. Clarence L. Haynes, Jr., "How Many Books are in the Bible and How Did They Get Chosen," biblestudytools.com, May 25, 2021, https://www.biblestudytools.com/bible-study/topical-studies/how-many-books-are-in-the-bible-and-how-did-they-get-there.html.

2. "How Many Chapters & Verses are in Each Book of the Bible," *Bible Memory Goal,* March 29, 2023, https://www.biblememorygoal.com/how-many-chapters-verses-in-the-bible.

3. "The Law, the Prophets, and the Psalms: How is the Old Testament Divided," *The Bible Made Plain,* December 20, 2021, https://thebiblemadeplain.com/the-law-the-prophets-and-the-psalms-how-is-the-old-testament-divided.

4. "What is the Bible Referring to when it Mentions the Law and the Prophets," *GotQuestions.org,* January 4, 2022, https://www.gotquestions.org/law-and-the-prophets.html.

5. Jeff A. Benner, "What is Torah," *Ancient Hebrew Research Center,* (n.d.), https://ancient-hebrew.org/studies-words/what-is-torah.htm.

6. *Merriam-Webster*, s.v. "Pentateuch (*n.*)," accessed October 1, 2023, https://www.merriam-webster.com/dictionary/Pentateuch.

7. "What is the Pentateuch," *GotQuestions.org,* January 4, 2022, https://www.gotquestions.org/Pentateuch.html.

CHAPTER 15: ROAD TRIP TO REDEMPTION

1. "C. S. Lewis as Atheist turned Apostle," *CSLewis.com*, May 2, 2012, https://www.cslewis.com/c-s-lewis-as-atheist-turned-apostle.gifts.

ABOUT THE AUTHOR

Jade Creighton is a Christian writer, musician, and worship leader. She lives in the Tampa Bay area with her husband and daughter.

For more information or to order this title, visit:
thesavedbook.com